SEEING LANGUAGE IN SIGN

THE WORK OF

Seeing

WILLIAM C. STOKOE

Language

BY JANE MAHER

in Sign

Foreword by Oliver Sacks

GALLAUDET UNIVERSITY PRESS   WASHINGTON, D.C.

Gallaudet University Press
Washington, DC 20002

Library of Congress Cataloging-in-Publication Data

Maher, Jane, 1947-
Seeing language in sign : the work of William C.
Stokoe / Jane Maher : foreword by Oliver Sacks
p. cm.

Includes bibliographical references and index.

ISBN: 1-56368-053-X (alk. paper)
ISBN: 1-56368-470-8 (alk. paper) softcover edition

1. Stokoe, William C. 2. Teachers of the deaf — United
States — Biography. 3. Linguists — United States —
Biography 4. American Sign Language. I. Title.

HV2534.S76M35 1996
419'.092-dc20
[B]

95-46906
CIP

♾ The paper used in this publication meets the minimum requirements of
American National Standard for Information Sciences—Permanence of Paper
for Printed Library Materials, ANSI Z39.48-1984.

FOR MY MOTHER

Anne Peronti

CONTENTS

FOREWORD

· · · · · · ·

I first met Bill Stokoe in December of 1986. I was nervous about meeting him: he was the man who had cracked American Sign Language (intellectually equivalent to cracking the Rosetta Stone, and emotionally, morally, infinitely more difficult because no one, least of all the deaf, thought of Sign as a real language until he did this), and I was a complete outsider — not deaf, not a linguist, not even capable of more than the most rudimentary signing. I had also heard that he was sometimes prickly, impatient, arrogant, a man of fierce and uncompromising forthrightness.

What I found was a man immensely humble, a man who felt he had been given far more than he had received, and he was immensely generous. I found him wonderfully, bracingly, direct and open — so immediate and candid and unguarded that my own diffidence and defenses, the armor with which one encases oneself for first encounters, melted away on the spot. We ranged over many different subjects, and I got an intense sense of the range, the delicacy, and the richness of his mind. A few days later he sent me a parcel of books — including his own, much annotated, personal copy of *Language Origins*; and I, in return, sent him the books I had written, with the hope that we might have future contact. There was this almost explosive feeling of giving and receiving from the start — there are no half-measures with a man like Bill Stokoe.

I got an enormous letter from him a few days later (Stokoe is a marvelous letter writer, as I was to find). In this first letter, he thought back on his early days at Gallaudet:

> Linguistics was getting pretty schematic. I found that Trager and Smith were making a promising integration in 1957, just when Chomsky purported to show that syntax was innate. Linguists became preoccupied with rules any computer

could follow, keeping individuals, interaction, society, and culture out of their descriptions of "the language organ" and its function. I find Chomsky the man charming but his linguistics deterministic and cold. I realized deaf people signing were using language not by discovering their generative rules but by seeing that they were acting like social beings. I still chafe at the mechanistic view too many sign language linguists take.

The passionate tone, the insistence on the human, cultural dimension of language, reminded me very much of the first letter I had got from the great neuropsychologist A. R. Luria, when he spoke of "the dry, mechanical thinking of my friend B. F. Skinner," and insisted that language arose through interaction, dialogically, between mother and child. Stokoe ended his letter, "This is just the first installment of that further contact you mention," and there then followed (in a way which delighted me — I am somewhat prone to such additions myself) a postscript three times as long as the letter, in a very different mode, a mode of the richest association and imagery. I had written a case history in *The Man Who Mistook his Wife for a Hat* on involuntary memories ("Reminiscence"), and this led Bill to speak of his own experience of such memories, the total way in which they could transport him:

> At first the moments of reminiscence, being transported into complete scenes, were easily identified: they happened just before falling asleep, just after waking, or post coitus. Later they flashed into my mind ad libitum, as I sat writing, paused in thought, as I was eating, driving, mowing the lawn. . . . There seems to be time always in most any activity to have my attention switched to these other places and times, as if consciousness had a special-effects generator feeding a split screen from one remote and one attached camera. There is no sensation of split, though. I can contemplate the where, who, what's happening, and more while fully aware of immediate surroundings.
>
> Sometimes at table I say to Ruth, for instance, "We're walking up to that street in Zurich where the bridge crosses and the Heimatwerk store is on the corner." She usually

replies, "How nice for you"; and it is. I am there and here at the same moment, and there is often a trip abroad or a delightful-to-relive experience any time these last 65 years. I have toyed with the possibility that subtle sense impressions are triggers. When the air is moist and fragrant with spring, or fall, vegetation (or in the shower, with the scent of Pears soap and damp curtain), I am back in England or Scotland in 1953–4, 61, 68, 72, 77. . . . When the air is keener, I am back on a hillside of the washed-out 98 acres my father bought in 1925 and reforested, in a particular spot, looking, it may be, at a devil's paintbrush or a red pine seedling that has a broken tip and a grouse dropping beside its gnarled stem.

But perhaps, Stokoe added, "links like that explain only a small part, if they do. Maybe like Walt Whitman I have learned how to loaf and invite my soul. . . . I am infinitely richer for these reminiscences."

Luria's first letter to me, after a rather formal presentation of his own intellectual history, moved into a different mode and related an astonishing story of his meeting with Pavlov: the old man (Pavlov was then in his eighties), looking like Moses, tore Luria's first book in half, flung the fragments at his feet, and yelled "You call yourself a scientist!" This startling episode was related by Luria with vividness and gusto in a way that brought out its comic and terrible aspects equally. He clearly had an almost novelistic gift for narrative, equal and complementary to his great scientific gifts — and this was evidently the case with Stokoe, too. I found myself wondering, after Stokoe's first letter, whether these two gifts, or dispositions, served to split him, distract him, or divide him, or whether they were somehow complementary, as they were with Luria.

One of the most moving chapters in Jane Maher's book brings to life and analyzes a most crucial period in Stokoe's life, the ten years following his arrival at Gallaudet. During this time he moved from being a teacher of English, an explicator of Chaucer, to becoming an explorer of the culture and language of deaf people, of their actual mode of communication.

Signing had been seen, up to this time, as a sort of pantomime or broken English on the hands — something without internal structure or coherence or rules, something far below the level of language. This view was not only near-universal among the hearing population, but was shared by most deaf people, too. It was this view that had led (following the notorious Milan conference of 1880) to the stamping out of sign in most schools for the deaf, relegating sign to an informal, sometimes ashamed, marginal existence. Stokoe, coming to Gallaudet as an outsider, without these ingrained biases, was quick to recognize the intelligence of his young students and the swiftness and efficiency of their forbidden, private signing. He saw its power as a tool, a vehicle for communication and culture. He had to suspect, despite universal doubt, that signing was a genuine language. He then turned to a minute examination of the act, the interactions, of signing itself — an examination made possible by his extraordinary powers of observation and analysis (to which he soon added cinematography and a frame-by-frame analysis of signing). He was now able to show that signs were not just pictorial or iconic, but, on the contrary, complex abstract symbols with an elaborate internal structure.

He was the first to look for a structure, to analyze signs, to dissect them, to search for constituent parts. He proposed that each sign had at least three independent parts — location, handshape, and movement (analogous to the phonemes of speech) — and that each part had a limited number of combinations. He delineated nineteen different handshapes, twelve locations, and twenty-four types of movements. These symbols, moreover, were linked in a syntax or grammar every bit as complex and complete as that of spoken language. In 1960 he published his groundbreaking paper, *Sign Language Structure*, and five years later (with his deaf colleagues Dorothy Casterline and Carl Croneberg) the monumental *Dictionary of American Sign Language on Linguistic Principles*. Signs in the dictionary were arranged not thematically (e.g., signs for food, signs for animals, etc.) but systematically, according to their parts and the organization and principles of the language. This work showed the lexical structure of language, the linguistic interrelatedness of a basic 3000 sign "words."

Writing of the *Dictionary* fifteen years later, Carol Padden, an early student of Stokoe's, and now an eminent deaf linguist, wrote: "It was unique to describe 'Deaf people' as constituting a cultural group . . . it represented a break from the long tradition of 'pathologizing' Deaf people. . . . In a sense the book brought official and public recognition of a deeper aspect of Deaf people's lives: their culture." But though in retrospect Stokoe's works were seen as "bombshells" or "landmarks," and though in retrospect they can be seen as having had a major part in leading to the subsequent transformation of consciousness, they were all but ignored at the time. Stokoe himself has commented: "Publication [of *Sign Language Structure*] brought a curious local reaction. With the exception of . . . one or two colleagues, the entire Gallaudet faculty rudely attacked me, linguistics, and the study of signing as a language."

There was certainly very little impact among his fellow linguists: the great general works on language of the 1960s make no reference to it — or indeed to sign language at all. More remarkable, in a sense, was the indifferent or hostile reaction of deaf people themselves, whom one might have thought would have been the first to see and welcome Stokoe's insights. But it was precisely signers who were most resistant to his notions. Thus Gil Eastman (later to become an acclaimed Deaf playwright and a most ardent supporter of Stokoe's) recalls, "My colleagues and I laughed at Dr. Stokoe and his crazy project. It was impossible to analyze our sign language."

Stokoe persevered in the face of all this, pursuing his studies with quiet stubbornness, even, when possible, turning adversities to advantage. Thus when his colleagues in the English Department replaced him as chairman in 1972, he was able to devote himself almost entirely to research, making the Linguistics Research Laboratory something more than the summer and spare time activity it had been for a dozen years. Here Stokoe and his students and collaborators continued their research. Many of his collaborators were themselves deaf, and this was the first time that deaf people had ever been employed as equals in fundamental research. Many of his students went on to specialize in linguistics, becoming the first generation of deaf

Sign linguists. Additionally, Stokoe founded a journal, *Sign Language Studies*, which provided a crucial forum for dissemination and discussion of the new knowledge.

Increasingly known and respected among linguists, educators, and Deaf people, Stokoe remained a pariah, or worse, in the eyes of Gallaudet's administration. Maher brings out the tremendous stubbornness in Stokoe's character — how this stubbornness and forthrightness constantly brought him into collision with others, above all, with the administration of the college, with their (often largely unconscious) depreciation of deaf people and signing; but how too it was a prerequisite to his great achievements, achieved in the face of near-universal discouragement. She brings out, too, the heroic quality of this time (a word which Stokoe, in his modesty, would never allow).

Maher describes vividly the most grievous chapter in Stokoe's professional life, with Gallaudet's closing in 1984 of the Linguistics Research Laboratory where Stokoe and his colleagues had labored so productively. Stokoe was then 65 and had devoted 29 years of his life to the college, 29 years of monumental contribution — and at this point when he should have been most honored, his lab was disbanded, and his beloved associates were flung out on their ears.

When I met him a couple of years later, he was still, I think, quite mortified and depressed, even though he had remained ceaselessly productive and active, lecturing, publishing, and encouraging others where he could no longer do research himself. And yet it was clear to Stokoe, as to many others at Gallaudet at this point, that deep change, and even revolution, was in the air; Stokoe's work, its continuity, its integrity, formed a sort of backdrop to this. The revolution of the deaf broke out in 1988 — the students at Gallaudet closed the university in protest against a new president who did not sign, who had no concept of what it meant to be deaf, or of Deaf language or identity, a protest which led, in five triumphant days, to the installation of a deaf president, I. King Jordan, the first in Gallaudet's history. Stokoe was crucially behind the candidacy of Jordan, whom he had known and respected for many years. The militancies of '88 paved the way to the cultural rebirth of 1989, the astonishing gathering in Washington of 7000 deaf people (and their eighty-odd sign languages) from all over the world for an unprecedented conference and grand festival of sign arts — The Deaf Way.

Stokoe himself gave a talk at The Deaf Way, and the whole gathering gave an extraordinary sense of a rounding and completion to the work he had started some thirty years before. Indeed, another person who had attended The Deaf Way told me that he had seen Stokoe, the previous day, walking very quietly through it all, with the slight, perhaps unconscious smile of a father. "Life has many bright moments," Stokoe wrote me later, "though few so overwhelming as The Deaf Way." In 1990, Gallaudet, making partial amends for its ousting of Stokoe just a few years before, awarded him an honorary doctor of letters degree in recognition of his central role in the elucidation and legitimation of American Sign Language.

But there were many grim moments too, for Stokoe's wife of forty years, Ruth, had started to show memory lapses, and was now on the tragic, downward path of Alzheimer's disease. He often spoke of what was happening to her, in his letters to me, with a passionate objectivity and a most tender, intimate apprehension of her own, now so greatly altered, emotions and states of mind; at once, inseparably, the observer and the lover.

Stokoe's appreciation of the subjective lies at the center of his own being, no less than the phenomenological, the theoretical, the mathematical. He came to Gallaudet, as a young man, to share his knowledge and passion for medieval poetry, for Chaucer. His earlier work had to do with deciphering Chaucer, understanding the meaning of certain previously obscure words and phrases. This required a huge knowledge of Middle English vocabulary and grammar, and of the poetic devices of the time; but it also required a penetration into Chaucer's subjectivity, his sensibilities, his consciousness, his mind; and an acute sense of what it must have been like to live in the fourteenth century, of what it must have meant to *be* Chaucer. Stokoe finally deciphered the words because he read Chaucer's mind, divined his intentions, *knew* exactly the meaning Chaucer wished to convey.

It was a similar blending of tremendous acuity in observing

the forms of a visual language (almost unimaginably alien to one steeped in speech), with a profoundly empathetic sense of content, of others' states of mind and intentions, that made it possible for Stokoe to establish the linguistic characteristics of American Sign Language — its grammatical intricacy, its delicacy of meaning.

Current morphologists of sign language have now gone far beyond Stokoe's pioneer work — so much so that he is sometimes seen as obsolete or old-fashioned. Yet, no "pure" morphologist, one feels, could ever have opened the door to a new mode of communication in the first place — and not only a mode of communication, but a mode of cognition, of sensibility, of identity too.

At 76, Bill Stokoe is as active and creative as ever; last year (with his colleagues David Armstrong and Sherman Wilcox) he brought out an audacious new book, *Gesture and the Nature of Language*, presenting the hypothesis (with impressive linguistic, neural, and ethological evidence to support it) that Sign might be not just a peculiar, specialized language developed by the deaf, but one of the universal, primordial forms of language achieved by our species.

Bill Stokoe has dedicated himself to Deaf people and the study of their language for forty years. He has opened, for all of us, a new era of understanding, and this has been possible because of his rare combination of scientific, humane, and poetic passions, and a spaciousness of mind that could integrate all of these. Stokoe is, I think, one of the most remarkable men of our time, and a comprehensive biography of him has been long overdue. I am delighted that, finally, it has been written.

Oliver Sacks

ACKNOWLEDGMENTS

. . . .

This book was originally written as a dissertation for the School of Education of New York University; I would like to thank my advisor (and friend) John Mayher, who helped me to realize the power of narrative as a tool to help educators understand the role they play in their students' lives, both in and outside the classroom. I am also grateful to Harold Vine and Sue Livingston, who served on my dissertation committee, for their careful and thoughtful responses to my work.

Much of the information contained in this biography was collected through interviews and correspondence with Bill Stokoe's friends and colleagues. They set aside time from extraordinarily busy schedules to help me understand the profundity and complexity of Stokoe's accomplishments. In particular, I thank George E. Detmold and Carl G. Croneberg.

Many thanks to Elena Marciante who spent long hours transcribing the taped interviews. Thank you to Ivey Pittle Wallace, managing editor at Gallaudet University Press, whose suggestions and comments (although I tried to resist) were accurate and insightful, and to Martha Yager, who edited the manuscript with skill and sensitivity.

As I approach the end of this long and sometimes difficult enterprise, I wonder whether there is any way to express my gratitude to Bill Stokoe. Did he realize what he was getting into when he returned my telephone call several years ago? Now that I know him, I think perhaps he did. After all, as a teacher and a scholar who has spent much of his adult life combatting the ignorance that surrounds deaf language and culture, it probably was not surprising that a graduate student who knew very little about linguistics and possessed limited skills in American Sign Language would have the audacity to ask to be his biographer. This private and modest man had to endure my questioning and probing. At the same time, he had to educate me so that I could better understand the discoveries and accomplishments that have earned him prominence and respect not only among linguists but among members of the deaf community — a relatively rare accomplishment for a hearing person.

It is tempting to resort to the vocabulary of eulogy to describe Bill Stokoe: brilliant, passionate, courageous; however, such words are powerless after all to capture the essence of this complex man. No biographer can tell a life fully and accurately, but I hope I have succeeded in telling enough about Bill Stokoe to enable others to know — at least a little better — of the rich, full, and productive life that he has lived.

. . . .

Photographs on the cover, frontispiece, and pages 40 and 79 courtesy of Gallaudet University Archives. Photographs on pages 1, 24, 58, 131, and top of 161 courtesy of William C. Stokoe. Photographs on page 6 reprinted from *The Dictionary of American Sign Language* by Stokoe, Casterline, and Croneberg (pp. xx, xxi). Photograph on page 101 courtesy of Robbin Battison. Photograph on bottom of page 161 by Chun Louie, courtesy of Gallaudet University Photography Services.

INTRODUCTION

· · · · · · ·

Bill Stokoe is the father of linguistics in the field of
American Sign Language. If it weren't for him, we'd still be
in the Dark Ages.

GIL EASTMAN

When the students of Gallaudet University shut down their campus in March of 1988, they were not simply protesting the appointment of a hearing president who knew only a few signs of American Sign Language and who was ignorant of the culture it expressed. They were protesting more than one hundred years of ignorance, oppression, and injustice. But in those one hundred years, not all hearing people had been the enemy; there had always been those who were able to see beyond the stereotypes, beyond the self-fulfilling prophecies. And while it must be stated emphatically that the Deaf President Now Revolution was conceived and conducted by deaf students and adults who were no longer willing to be treated as an oppressed minority, recognition must be given to those who helped them and other deaf Americans to realize that their signs, which had been "actively banished by the hearing establishment concerned with the deaf for over a century," constituted a unique and fully developed language.[1]

One of the first people to see signing as a legitimate language was a Gallaudet English professor, Dr. William C. Stokoe, Jr., hired in 1955 to teach – of all things – Chaucer. Although some of the students who participated in the Deaf President Now Revolution may never even have heard of Bill Stokoe (pronounced "stow-key"), those who do know of his work recognize its connection to the successful efforts now under way by deaf people for total control of their education, of their language, of their lives. In the words of Lou Fant, the well-known actor, writer, and interpreter,

Bill made the first crack in the dam that eventually erupted into the flood that we call deaf empowerment. Without a legitimately recognized language, there is no culture; without a culture, there is no self-identity; without self-identity, you just go on trying to be what others demand you be. Without the concept of deaf culture and the identity that goes with it, there would have been no Deaf President Now [DPN]. The chain of events that led to the DPN protest had its first link forged by none other than Bill. Not only can you safely connect Bill's work to the DPN protest . . . you can't leave it out; it's sort of the culmination, the crowning achievement of his work. It's what his work was all about. Bill didn't just discover a language, he laid the foundation for most of what's happened to empower deaf people and gain them the access they deserve.[2]

Fant is not alone in praising Stokoe. Gil Eastman, the deaf actor and playwright, has called him "The Father of Sign Language Linguistics."[3] There is not one publication dealing with American Sign Language written after 1965 that does not contain at least one reference to his work, and in the growing number of American Sign Language courses being taught, the chances are excellent that during the introduction Bill Stokoe's name will be mentioned. Experts in deaf education have compared what Stokoe did for American Sign Language to the pioneering work of geniuses such as Galileo, Copernicus, and Einstein. "In his quiet, unassuming way," Fant observes, "he unleashed forces that have reshaped our world without meaning to or even realizing that he was doing it."[4]

Yet little is known about Bill Stokoe. He is always amused by the reaction of people who hear his voice when they dial Linstok Press, a small publishing company specializing in sign language studies, which until May 1991 he directed from his home: "They're surprised that I'm even alive, much less speaking to them on the phone."[5] It shouldn't be this way. The story of Bill Stokoe's life and work should be told, not just for those interested in deaf language, culture, and education, but for anyone interested in the way one man used his courage, his brilliance, and his tenacity to help others. Harlan Lane, author of *When the Mind Hears*, explains that Stokoe "started a worldwide movement of scholarship, contributed significantly to the liberation of minorities throughout the world, [and] has students both hearing and deaf now carrying the flame around the globe."[6]

What follows is an attempt to tell Bill Stokoe's story. Despite his modesty, he is willing that the story be told. ("I can hardly believe that someone has lighted on me as a subject," he says.)[7] His friends and associates are far more enthusiastic. Scores of them were willing to spend enormous time and energy to provide the information needed to tell of his extraordinary life.

I could not talk to the person who knows Bill Stokoe best, however. Ruth Stokoe, his wife of more than fifty years, suffers from Alzheimer's disease. Ruth Stokoe and the people who use American Sign Language are Bill Stokoe's two great passions. During the thirty years that he spent teaching and learning at Gallaudet University, Ruth Stokoe cared for their two children and encouraged him when most others thought his research into American Sign Language was absurd, even dangerous. It is indicative of their devotion to each other that during the Deaf President Now Revolution, a revolution sparked in large part by his work, Stokoe did not go to the Gallaudet campus as so many others did. He kept his television on day and night to follow the proceedings, and although he "was certainly there in spirit," he remained at home with Ruth, "where [he] was needed."[8]

During the course of his career at Gallaudet, Bill Stokoe was ridiculed and reviled by many of the people with whom he worked, both hearing and deaf — a fact that many would just as soon forget now that he has begun to receive the honor and recognition he so richly deserves. The citation that was presented to Stokoe by the president and the Board of Trustees of Gallaudet University when they awarded him an honorary degree on May 14, 1988, lauds him as a "pioneer" who

> belongs to that small handful of rare individuals who dared to deviate from the beaten trail. At the risk of his professional career he chose to take the turn to new and uncharted pathways.
>
> A scholar of Old and Middle English, his academic odyssey carried him from Cornell University to Wells College, to the University of Edinburgh, and eventually to Gallaudet as chairman of the English Department. In 1960 he began his controversial studies into the linguistic nature of American Sign Language, a venture which was initially met with scorn, skepticism, and little support from his colleagues.
>
> In time, his perseverance sparked a flame which reached all corners of the world, brought new insights into how deaf people communicate, opened doors, and created unprecedented waves in international schools of linguistics. He has brought to the sign language of every nation a needed measure of recognition and dignity.
>
> In 1971 Dr. Stokoe became director of the newly estab-

lished Linguistics Research Lab at Gallaudet and in 1972 launched a new journal, *Sign Language Studies*. At the centennial convention of the National Association of the Deaf in 1980, he was presented with a *Festschrift* — a celebration of writing — in the form of a book of essays in his honor, *Sign Language and the Deaf Community*.

Today, Gallaudet University honors William C. Stokoe, a man of vision and courage, who has helped immeasurably in reducing the bonds of cultural and language oppression among deaf people, and whose scholarly contribution to the field will be remembered in the years to come.[9]

Much is said in that citation, but much is also omitted. On the day that Stokoe received his honorary degree, he sat on the stage with some of the very same colleagues who had, during his many years at Gallaudet, treated him with the "scorn and skepticism" so conveniently left unexplained in the citation.

Through interviews and correspondence with Bill Stokoe, his family, his students and colleagues, his friends and foes; through reading his many essays, reviews, and speeches; through research of the many books and essays that have been written about deaf people and their language; through research at Gallaudet University and many other institutions; and through correspondence with linguists in five countries, I have collected enough information to present the story of an indomitable man — one who labored for a large period of his professional life with little or no support from his colleagues, from the Gallaudet administrators, from deaf people who disagreed with his theories. Bill Stokoe proved them wrong. It took almost thirty years, but Stokoe's work has shown that deaf people have their own language and culture, a language and culture that are different from — but equal to — those of hearing people.

When I. King Jordan, the first deaf president of Gallaudet University, agreed to help me in this endeavor, he wrote me a letter. "Do a good job," he urged. "Bill Stokoe is a giant in this field. He's not only a giant in this field, but he's a giant of a person. There's not enough I can say about the guy; I truly love him. I hope your work reflects that."[10]

I hope so, too.

CHAPTER I

. . . .

*The debate between signers and oralists is an old one, and it was
already old when Bell and Gallaudet assumed leadership of the two
ideological armies.*

RICHARD WINEFIELD *Never the Twain Shall Meet*

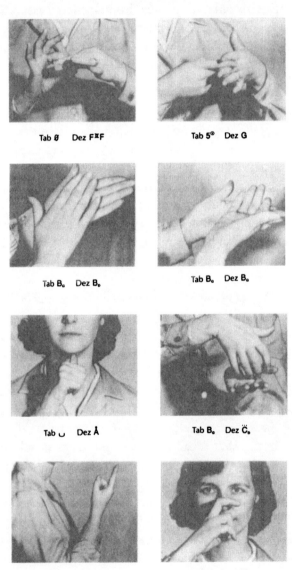

Tab Ø   Dez FᵡF   Tab 5[⊙]   Dez G

Tab B˳   Dez B˳   Tab B˳   Dez B˳

Tab ᴗ   Dez Å   Tab B˳   Dez C̈˳

Tab Ø   Dez √G˳   Tab ⌃   Dez V̈

The story of the introduction of sign language into the United States and its use in educating deaf people is well known, and it is synonymous with the name of Thomas Hopkins Gallaudet. In 1807, after graduating from Yale at the age of eighteen, Gallaudet studied law in Hartford. After only one year, however, he returned to Yale, where he studied English literature and became deeply engrossed in religious matters and the condition of his own soul. He soon decided that a career in business would help to improve his feeble health, but by 1813 he had abandoned business and enrolled in the Andover Theological Seminary. It was at this time that Thomas Hopkins Gallaudet first met Alice Cogswell, a seven-year-old deaf child, and immediately developed an interest in her welfare and education.

Alice's father, Mason Cogswell, a wealthy Hartford resident, had devoted enormous time and energy to finding a suitable way to educate not only his own daughter but other deaf children in Connecticut. Initially, Cogswell contacted the Scottish educator Thomas Braidwood, Jr., who was visiting the United States. The Braidwood family had earned a reputation in Europe for their success in using oral methods to educate deaf children. Braidwood had left Scotland to escape creditors and was in the process of establishing a school in Maryland. However, he was soon arrested for spending the money given to him as tutoring fees without having provided the tutoring services. His subsequent legal problems forced him to honor contracts in Virginia, preventing him from establishing a school or tutoring in the Hartford area.

This was fortuitous not only for Alice Cogswell but for the future of deaf education in the United States. Gallaudet, while still a student at Andover, began to tutor Alice, and his success in this endeavor — combined with Braidwood's continuing problems with debtors — led Cogswell and other prominent Hartford residents to choose Gallaudet to travel to Europe in 1815 to research the methods being used there to educate deaf children. On his return Gallaudet applied these methods in a school established by his Hartford patrons.

It is somewhat ironic that Gallaudet, whose name has become so closely associated with sign language instruction, initially intended to visit the Braidwood School in Edinburgh, where oral instruction was espoused and practiced. The Braidwoods had always been secretive about their methods; the elder Braidwood had once offered to publicize his methods only if he were rewarded financially by the European nobility. Gallaudet was unable to gain permission to study with the Braidwood family. At about the same time, he accidentally encountered the Abbé Sicard, director of the Royal Institution for the Deaf in Paris, where the sign language that had been developed by the school's founder, Charles-Michel de l'Épée, "the father of the Deaf," was being used to teach deaf students. Sicard had traveled to England from Paris to exhibit the accomplishments of his two star pupils, Jean Massieu and Laurent Clerc. Sicard, like his predecessor, the Abbé de l'Épée, was willing to share his methods of instruction with others.

Thomas Hopkins Gallaudet traveled to Paris and began to observe and participate in the instruction the deaf pupils were receiving at the school. He wrote to Cogswell with great enthusiasm: "I have already learned the signs of most of the tenses of the verbs in all their moods and in all their varieties. . . . Don't be alarmed at this system of signs. A great deal of it is truly valuable and will very much accelerate the progress of my scholars."[1]

After only a few months, Gallaudet (who was already homesick) was convinced that the French method of manual signing was the one he wanted to bring back to the United States. As a result, rather than remain in Paris to continue his studies and training, he persuaded Laurent Clerc to return with him to Hartford to help establish the first school for deaf pupils in the United States.

The school officially opened in 1817 and was called The American Asylum for the Education and Instruction of Deaf and Dumb Persons. (Today it is known as the American School for the Deaf.) Alice Cogswell was registered as the first pupil; she was soon joined by and became a close friend of nineteen-year-old Sophia Fowler, who would become Gallaudet's wife four years later.

The Connecticut legislature appropriated funds for the school, and soon after, the United States granted a 23,000-acre site to the school. Student enrollment rose steadily; in 1819 the

Massachusetts legislature agreed to pay the expenses of twenty deaf students from Massachusetts; New Hampshire, Maine, Vermont, and Rhode Island soon followed with appropriations for students from their states.

Although Gallaudet and Clerc worked excruciatingly long and hard hours, although there were often administrative and political problems, and although Gallaudet and Clerc were often confused by the differences between them — one was deaf and had been raised in Paris, the other was hearing and had been raised in puritanical New England and trained in a theological seminary — their work together resulted in immediate success. More and more deaf students enrolled in the school, and other states modeled programs for the deaf after the Hartford school.

However, articulation and speechreading methods were also being employed in the United States, particularly in those schools founded by the Braidwoods in Virginia and in the Hopkinsville School established in Kentucky by Robert T. Anderson. The debate between proponents of oralism and sign language (also known as "manual communication") was not yet the divisive issue it would later become; in fact, the American School was the first in the United States to employ a full-time speech teacher. This decision was probably based more on pragmatic than philosophical considerations, however; it was an attempt to prevent oralists from establishing a school in Massachusetts that would compete for many of the same students attending the Hartford school.[2]

Ironically, oralism gained a strong foothold in this country for almost precisely the same reason that sign language was introduced — the concern of a father for his deaf daughter. Mabel Hubbard, the daughter of a prominent Massachusetts citizen, Gardiner Greene Hubbard, had lost her hearing at the age of five as a result of scarlet fever. Her father was reluctant to have her attend the "manual" school in Hartford and instead had her educated orally at home, where Alexander Graham Bell was one of her tutors. Her progress was so encouraging that Hubbard decided to establish an oral school. With hard work, the support of the governor of Massachusetts, and financial backing from John Clarke, the Clarke School for Deaf Mutes was established in Northampton, Massachusetts, in 1867.

Mabel Hubbard would later marry Alexander Graham Bell, whose support of oralism enabled its adherents to gain enormous power and control over the education of deaf people in the United States.

Biographers, educators, and historians have written extensively about the rift that eventually developed between Thomas Hopkins Gallaudet's son, Edward Miner Gallaudet (who continued his father's work), and Alexander Graham Bell. Richard Winefield's account, *Never the Twain Shall Meet*, shows that the clash was almost inevitable given the life experiences of these two men. Both had deaf mothers who had thrived under different methods of instruction. And both had strong, dedicated fathers who had blazed different trails for their sons.

Thomas Hopkins Gallaudet was married to Sophia Fowler, one of his deaf students, who had lost her hearing too early in life to develop speech. Sophia had progressed academically with exposure to manual signing, although she never learned to read and write very well, having received no formal education before the age of nineteen. Gallaudet had immediately recognized her intelligence and admired her beauty, and their long, happy marriage was testimony to Gallaudet's comfort and confidence in signing as a means of communication. Sophia Fowler Gallaudet was never entirely comfortable in hearing society, but she succeeded brilliantly as a homemaker and mother and, in middle age, as matron of her son's college. She and Gallaudet had four sons and four daughters.

Thomas Hopkins Gallaudet remained devoted to deaf education until his death in 1851, and his son Edward Miner Gallaudet, after a brief career in banking, continued the tradition. Edward recalled that he was twelve years old when his father suggested that "perhaps I might like to take up the work which had engaged the energies of his early manhood. He spoke at some length of the joy he had in doing what he believed was his Master's work when he labored for the deaf and said he believed I would never be sorry if I carried out his suggestion."[3]

Edward Miner Gallaudet was only twenty years old in 1857 when he assumed leadership of the Columbia Institution for the Deaf and Dumb and the Blind in Washington, D.C. (A college was added to the institution in 1864, named Gallaudet College after his father and subsequently changed to Gallaudet University.) The school was funded entirely by the United States government. When Edward Miner Gallaudet was offered the directorship of the school, his contract stipulated that his mother, Sophia Fowler Gallaudet, serve as matron — evidence of the respect she had earned in the deaf community. She served admirably, winning the reverence and love of the faculty and students. Throughout his life, Edward Miner Gallaudet was surrounded by deaf people who led full, productive lives as a result of using the sign language that his father and Laurent Clerc had brought back from France.

Like Edward Miner Gallaudet, Alexander Graham Bell was strongly influenced by his parents. His mother, Eliza Bell, had lost much of her hearing as a child. Although she could not read lips, she was able to speak well. She was extremely well read and was even able to educate her children at home. Alexander Graham Bell's father, Alexander Melville Bell, dedicated his life to Visible Speech, a system he developed in an attempt to improve hearing people's speech patterns and elocution. He published numerous books on the topic and gave public lectures and tours, often using his sons to demonstrate his techniques. The Visible Speech system provided a logical foundation for Alexander Graham Bell's firm belief in oralism, a belief that he never abandoned. Long before Bell became famous for his invention of the telephone, he had developed what would become a lifelong interest in teaching deaf students. He had even started his own school in Boston, The School of Vocal Physiology and Elocution, where he used his father's methods and charts to teach deaf children the meanings of Visible Speech symbols; however, the school closed for lack of students. He later used his wealth and prominence to establish an organization whose prime purpose was to advocate and support the oral movement in the United States.

Bell found confirmation of his beliefs in the success of his wife's oral training. Mabel Hubbard Bell had excellent speech skills. As Winefield explains, it was initially believed that she had lost her hearing as a very young child. Many years later, in 1919, it was discovered through family letters that she had lost her hearing at the age of five, *after* her speech had developed, and that she had never completely lost the ability to speak. Unaware of the truth, Bell used his wife as an example of the success of the oral method, which he defended for more than forty years. As Winefield observes, "His conviction may well have been weakened had he known the true nature and extent of his wife's hearing loss."[4]

Eventually, as the debate between the proponents of sign language and oralism grew more heated and divisive, Edward Miner Gallaudet and Alexander Graham Bell came to be seen as the primary representatives and supporters of their respective methods. It was almost inevitable that, despite occasional attempts to come to some sort of compromise, the two men ultimately stopped communicating with each other; their philosophical differences were simply too great for them to coexist. As Winefield explains,

> Bell and Gallaudet disagreed over what constituted normal behavior and normal society and how deaf people fit into that society. Bell believed normal meant being as much like hearing people as possible. Deaf people could become active, fulfilled members of society if they could communicate like hearing people. Gallaudet equated normal with educational attainment and moral development. With the proper intellectual and moral training, deaf people could find themselves happy and productive members of society.[5]

The differences in the two men's interests — and influence — can most clearly be seen through their activities. Edward Miner Gallaudet never wavered in his advocacy of the use of sign language; one of the first teachers he hired upon assuming directorship of the Washington, D.C., school was James Dennison, a deaf man who had been educated at the American School for Deaf-Mutes in Hartford. Gallaudet devoted enormous time and energy to the school itself; he recorded in his memoirs having once sought medical treatment "growing out of the pressure of my many cares and responsibilities."[6]

One of his primary responsibilities was to ensure that Congress continued to fund the school. In his memoir, *History of the College for the Deaf, 1857–1907*, Gallaudet reprinted the following description of his activities that appeared in the *Washington*

Union (January 22, 1858). This passage and his decision to re-print it indicate not only his dedication to the school but also the pride he took in the way the deaf students were able to learn and communicate through sign language.

> The noble old hall of the House of Representatives was lighted up last evening. . . . It was the first public exhibition of the pupils of the Columbia Institution for the Instruction of the Deaf and Dumb and the Blind, who entered at the appointed hour neatly dressed and took seats around the Speaker's rostrum. . . . Among the large audience there were many members of Congress, clergymen, and distinguished citizens, with several deaf-mutes, who kept their fingers busi-ly occupied with their pantomime comments on the scene. E. M. Gallaudet, Esq., the Principal of the Institution, deliv-ered a brief, sensible, and eloquent address. He reviewed the gradual creation of institutions for the education of the deaf and dumb, and of the blind, in the various states, and then urged the claims of the institution here, which has been for-warded, and sustained, by individual liberality, and now asks the aid of Congress.
>
> Vocal and instrumental music followed, after which the deaf-mutes gave representations of various passions, senti-ments, etc., in obedience to the signs of their preceptor. A little fellow's personification of a snow storm was very comi-cal, and a young girl's idea of an angel was extremely touch-ing. Exercises on the blackboard followed, in which some of the pupils evinced great proficiency in their studies. . . . The exhibition can but add to the deep sympathy already felt for the institution.[7]

The congressmen were sufficiently impressed to allot the additional money requested by Edward Miner Gallaudet. And several years after the college had been chartered, when a mem-ber of the House Committee on Appropriations suggested that funding for building at Gallaudet be withheld, "shoulders shook with laughter" when it was hoped that "any gentleman who undertakes to open his mouth in opposition to this appropria-tion 'may be struck dumb.'"[8] (To this day, the United States government continues to fund Gallaudet University.)

In 1870 Gallaudet announced in his annual report the career plans of the first three graduates of the college: "One in the service of the Patent Office; one to instruct his fellow mutes in Illinois; and the third to supply a professor's place, as tutor, in the college from which he has just graduated."[9] The report reflected precisely what Gallaudet and his father had always known: that deaf students educated through manual sign language could develop the skills and the knowledge necessary to lead productive and fulfilling lives, particularly in the service of other deaf people. The graduation was the culmination of the work that had begun when Thomas Hopkins Gallaudet returned to the United States with Laurent Clerc.

However, Edward Miner Gallaudet never rejected the possibility of the use of oral methods if they could enhance the educational achievements of deaf students. On his return in 1867 from a tour of European schools, he presented a detailed report to the board of the college. In the report he observed that in the European schools, "the intellectual and moral development of the pupil [was] deemed to be the true aim in his education, the sign language being regarded as an instrument only to do this, and articulation as a valuable means of communication between the deaf-mute and his hearing-speaking fellows, the imparting of which should be attempted in all cases when success is reasonably to be expected."[10] In 1868, when Gallaudet called for a meeting of all principals of day and residential schools to be held at his school, he included "the officers of the then newly started oral schools in Massachusetts and New York."[11]

Bell, on the other hand, convinced that he was doing what was best for deaf people, devoted his energies to securing an acceptance of oralism in the United States with the purpose of eliminating all sign language. Ignoring the fact that many deaf people perceived their deafness as a condition, not an affliction, he once said to a deaf audience: "You have to live in a world of hearing and speaking people, and everything that will help you to mingle with hearing and speaking people will promote your welfare and happiness."[12]

Furthermore, Bell had become interested in eugenics, and many of his ideas were deeply offensive to deaf people, particularly his belief that they should not intermarry. "It is the duty of every good man and every good woman to remember that children follow marriage," he wrote, "and I am sure that there is no one among the deaf who desires to have his affliction handed down to his children."[13]

In 1884 Bell headed a committee to plan for a major convention in New York City, the Convention of Articulation Teachers of the Deaf. It was agreed that the following topics would be addressed — topics which represented nothing less than an attempt to eradicate the use of sign language in deaf day and residential schools:

1. First steps in articulation teaching
2. Voice training
3. Speech reading
4. Classification of the deaf in regard to articulation teaching
5. Artificial aids to hearing
6. How best to make speech the vernacular of our pupils
7. Difficulties experienced by deaf articulators on account of the irregularities of English spelling
8. Articulation as a means of instruction
9. Prerequisites of teachers of articulation
10. History of the methods of teaching speech to the deaf
11. The best means of promoting the cause of articulation teaching in America[14]

On the last day of the convention, Alexander Graham Bell concluded his address to the hundreds of teachers who attended with an optimistic statement: "I am sure that we must all feel intense gratification that the results of this convention promise to be productive of so much good. I think we must all feel stimulated and encouraged by contact with one another, and I am sure that we shall go home with a deeper and firmer resolution to do what we can to give speech to the dumb and to teach the deaf to understand the speech of others."[15]

Bell's advocacy of oralism in the United States was mirrored in Europe. In 1880 at an international conference in Milan on the education of deaf children, it was decided, despite the protests of Gallaudet and a few other sign language advocates, that oralism should replace manual signing as the preferred method of communication in the education of the deaf. The advocates of oralism in the classroom at the Milan Conference perceived themselves as crusaders with nothing less than the spiritual and temporal welfare of deaf people at stake. One speaker at the conference declared:

> Oral speech is the sole power that can rekindle the light God breathed into man when, giving him a soul in a corporeal body, he gave him also a means of understanding, of conceiving, and of expressing himself. . . . While, on the one hand, mimic signs are not sufficient to express the fullness of thought, on the other they enhance and glorify fantasy and all the faculties of the sense of imagination. . . . The fantastic language of signs exalts the senses and foments the passions, whereas speech elevates the mind much more naturally, with calm, prudence and truth and avoids the danger of exaggerating the sentiment expressed and provoking harmful mental impressions.[16]

The decision made in Milan in 1880 to ban sign in favor of oralism aided Bell's crusade in the United States, where the tide clearly began to turn in his favor. As Winefield notes, although Gallaudet described the conference in Milan as a "stacked deck," it "gave the oral movement considerable credibility and infused its leaders with an almost messianic belief in the rightness of their approach."[17]

In 1887 Bell founded the Volta Bureau (later named the Alexander Graham Bell Association for the Deaf) in Washington, D.C., and the organization soon began to publish the *Volta Review*, a journal that celebrated the successes of oralism, particularly in schools. Although Gallaudet, always concerned with his students' welfare, was willing to employ a combined method of oralism and signing in deaf education if it would help students to learn better, Bell would not modify his position. He continued to use his wealth and influence to support oralism in schools; he even lobbied Congress to oppose funding for teachers being trained to use both oral and manual methods in the classroom. By the turn of the century, the split in this country was complete — and irrevocable. Despite the protests of most deaf people, and despite the efforts of Edward Miner Gallaudet and his supporters, oralism gained such a foothold in America that by 1927, probably the height of pure oralism in this country, sign had been almost completely banned from classrooms, except in the case of "oral failures." As more and more schools adopted the oralist-only approach, deaf teachers' prospects for employment became "so bad . . . that Gallaudet College openly discouraged deaf students from considering a teaching career."[18]

The elimination of deaf teachers was one of Bell's most important aims. In his *Memoir Upon the Formation of a Deaf Variety of the Human Race* (published in 1884), he observed that "nearly one-third of the teachers of the deaf . . . in America are themselves deaf, and this must be considered as another element favorable to the formation of a deaf race — to be therefore avoided."[19] Bell and his followers aspired to nothing less than the total dismantling of any institution that enabled deaf students to gather together, for he believed that such gatherings would encourage intermarrying, and he had erroneously concluded that deaf people who married were highly likely to produce deaf offspring.

Bell and his followers — and there were many of them, including some of the most influential eugenicists of the time — refused to acknowledge the utter failure of oralism (and the concomitant prohibition of sign language) in the classroom. As long as sign language was permitted to flourish in the United States, as long as it was used as the primary language in schools for the deaf, deaf people were able to thrive socially, academically, and culturally. The very fact that a special college had been founded for deaf students was testimony to the success teachers were having in educating deaf students through the use of their own sign language. However, by the turn of the century oralism so dominated deaf education in this country that many deaf people feared "the sign language" would be lost forever.[20]

Study after study confirmed the dismal results of oralism. Jerome Schein, in *At Home Among Strangers*, an account of the deaf community in the United States, cited more than nineteen studies and surveys (conducted over a fifty-year period) showing that, within twenty years of the acceptance of oralism in the United States, "deaf students were leaving school after twelve or more years with educational achievements far below the national averages." Schein pointed out that this had not always been the case:

> At the start of this century, hearing and deaf students went on to college at about the same rate, which proved the feasibility of Edward M. Gallaudet's idealistic thinking. But within a few years, college admissions for the general population rapidly accelerated, while those for the Deaf population remained nearly constant. By 1950, the ratio climbed to over 8.5 to 1 — students in the general population attended college over 8 times more often than deaf students.[21]

L. S. Vygotsky, the Russian psychologist whose theories have had a profound impact on educational practices, observes that

> The acquisition of language can provide a paradigm for the entire problem of the relation between learning and development. Language arises initially as a means of communication between the child and the people in his environment. Only subsequently, upon conversion to internal speech, does it come to organize the child's thought, that is, become an internal mental function.[22]

This theory has obvious implications for deaf children being taught in a language they are not biologically suited to understand or employ while being deprived of access to a language that is entirely suitable to their biological characteristics. Yet oralists refused to recognize the cognitive deprivation resulting from the implementation of their theories; they continued to espouse the philosophy of oralism, which "declares deafness as something that must be overcome,"[23] and insisted that their methods offered the only proper preparation "for a full life in the hearing society."[24] When deaf students, as a result of the cognitive deprivation of oralism, performed dismally on achievement tests, in the classroom, and in the workforce, and when they chose to associate with other deaf people rather than struggle to comprehend and be comprehended in a hearing society, the oralists nodded knowingly: such behavior simply bore out what they had said all along. James Woodward, a sociolinguist who specializes in the study of sign languages, explains that in the oralists' view, "deaf people who identif[ied] with the deaf community [were] isolated pathological handicapped individuals."[25] The oralists looked for medical cures or technological solutions, for they could never fathom, much less accept, the fact that deaf people not only desired but were capable of living lives "designed by themselves rather than those imposed by others."[26]

Not only had deaf people been deprived of the use of their own language, but control over their education had been taken over by people who did not even know their language, much less recognize and appreciate its value and beauty. As a result of these conditions, deaf people came to be viewed as deficient or handicapped, needing help and guidance. Jerome Schein explains that, until the 1960s, "the Deaf community accepted the general community's view of deafness as a pathological condition. From that it followed that education should strive to make deaf children as much like hearing children as possible. The curriculum naturally reflected these views."[27]

Nowhere are such views more apparent than in *The Psychology of Deafness*, written in 1957 by the psychologist Helmer R. Myklebust. For years this book was the standard training text at schools of education for teachers of deaf students. Although Myklebust was hearing, he felt fully qualified to inform others of "the provocative and intriguing ramifications of sensory deprivation."[28]

Myklebust warned his readers of "the probability that such a handicap might preclude actualization of true intellectual potential because of limited language." He claimed that deaf children were unable to perform on tests that require certain types of abstraction and reasoning processes. He noted inferior memory abilities in deaf children. He observed a similarity between deaf children and brain-damaged children in engaging in "concrete behavior." He perceived inferior abstract reasoning processes in deaf children, a "verbal language limitation which deafness imposes," an "effect of deafness on divergent thinking and evaluation ability," an isolation caused by deafness, an inability to integrate experience, and a possibility that "the personality might be less structured, more immature, less subtle, and more sensorimotor in character."

Myklebust also saw a reliance among deaf leaders "on admiration [more] than on organization and direction of activities"; he claimed that these same leaders were "more immature emotionally" and that all deaf, whether leaders or not, were "more aggressive and competitive." They had "greater emotional problems," he warned; he observed that deafness "feminizes the male and masculinizes the female." He determined that inferences could "only be made with caution" about the "intricate relationship between deafness and psychosexual adjustment." Some test scores, he said, indicated "unusually high incidence indicating maladjustment"; other scales were "indicative of psychotic behavior." He noted that "the deviant emotional and social behavior reported in studies of deaf children [had] persisted into adulthood, even among those who made a successful societal adjustment," and that "the characteristic pattern was one of being rigid, concrete, and socially and emotionally immature." Myklebust provided four chapters of such "provocative data."[29]

Toward the middle of the book, a 423-page text replete with graphs, charts, tables, and writing samples, Myklebust asserted that, "despite the fact that the deaf showed greater emotional disorder than the hard of hearing, the deaf seemed largely unaware of deafness as a handicap. In this regard they lacked insight into the significance of hearing." Myklebust then begrudgingly concluded that deafness "does not cause mental illness" but that "the personality pattern which emerges is a feeling of severe isolation and detachment with aggressive, almost desperate attempts to compensate and thereby maintain interpersonal contacts."[30]

We are told in the section on the evaluation of drawings done by deaf children compared with drawings done by normal children that Myklebust himself developed a modified version of the Drawing of the Human Figure Test especially "for use in the National Study of the psychology of deafness." Myklebust found that deaf children drew larger figures than "normal" children; that their drawings were "more naive, less mature, and more primitive perceptually"; that they portrayed "the male figure in a more frail, effeminate manner"; that deaf children in residential schools drew noses with nostrils more often than deaf children in day schools; that male deaf children drew more teeth than female deaf children; and that deaf female children drew hair "more frequently than males." And since deaf children drew ears "proportionately too large as compared to the 'normal'" children, Myklebust could only conclude that "developmentally, psychodynamically, and in terms of body image these children were more perceptually aware of the ear."[31]

Because the deaf children in residential schools didn't learn speech and lipreading but, rather, employed "the manual sign language," which Myklebust believed could not "be considered comparable to a verbal symbol system," those children "portrayed hands as being too large in comparison with the [deaf] day school subjects." Myklebust also observed that deaf children drew their figures with clubbed feet; and, as if that weren't bad enough, the residential children made the feet too big.

In the area of motor functioning, Myklebust noted that "deaf children are inferior to the hearing on locomotor coordination as measured by the Railwalking test." His conclusion: "An intensive program of remedial physical education seems not only warranted but urgently indicated." One study indicated that the deaf were equal to or superior to their hearing counterparts in social maturity; Myklebust advised that the study be viewed "with caution, because of the small sample involved."[32]

Myklebust found many "implications" in his studies "for training and adjustment." He was convinced that the deaf must learn to "accept dependency"; that the success of their training programs depends on the "extent to which [the programs] are focused on the specifics of the psychology of deafness," given "basic factors such as altered perceptual processes, altered memory, and disturbances of ego development."[33]

Myklebust insisted that "it is principally through words that we manipulate experience and are able to communicate with others." Given this, his conclusion is no surprise: "The child with deafness from infancy has a marked retardation in all aspects of language. Furthermore, no educational methodology known has been highly successful in overcoming this limitation. We must infer that when auditory language is lacking or seriously impeded, read and written language are restricted on a reciprocal basis."[34]

And in a declaration that would have made Alexander Graham Bell proud, Myklebust proclaimed:

Although speechreading has limitations as compared to auditory language, we must assume that it is the most suitable receptive language system when deafness is present. If speechreading were taught as the basic language, the deaf child would learn to comprehend the spoken word through this means, and it would constitute his basic inner language system. He would "think" in words, but not in auditory words. Nor would he think in visual-tactual ideographic images such as characterize the language of signs. His inner language would consist of words as they appear on the lips when spoken. Instead of vowel and consonant sounds, instead of pitch, inflection, and intonation, his words [would] consist of movement, form, shape, color, and other visually observable characteristics and attributes.[35]

For those who wondered whether sign could ever be used to teach speech and lipreading, Myklebust warned that

The manual sign language used by the deaf is an Ideographic language. . . . An Ideographic language characteristically uses a part of the object to represent the whole object. There are many examples of this in the sign language. Essentially it is more pictorial, less symbolic and as a system is one which falls mainly at the level of imagery. Ideographic language systems, in comparison with verbal symbol systems, lack precision, subtlety, and flexibility. It is likely that Man cannot achieve his ultimate potential through an Ideographic language, inasmuch as it is limited to the more concrete aspects of his experience. Comparatively, a verbal language is more abstract. Moreover, an adequate language system must include a written form. Although most Ideographic forms of language can be written, it is highly impractical to do so. In the case of the sign language it seems impossible to devise a written form. [William Stokoe devised such a form in his *Dictionary of American Sign Language*.] The manual sign system must be viewed as being inferior to the verbal as a language.[36]

Finally, in a chapter entitled "Interest Patterns, Aptitudes,

Special Abilities," Myklebust noted that the range of vocational choices by females was remarkably limited. "The three most common choices [of interest] were teaching, clerical, and housewife." But Myklebust was conducting his research in the mid-1950s, the height of the "Father Knows Best" era. Did he think that, had these females been hearing, they would have chosen physics, neurosurgery, and space exploration? Myklebust was relieved that the deaf women had chosen such "realistic" interests; he suggested that "their choices may reflect unconscious awareness that opportunities are limited or that deafness imposes a major limitation as far as many types of work are concerned."[37]

Boys didn't fare much better in Myklebust's study. After administering "the Stenquist Mechanical Aptitude Test, Test I; the Minnesota Paper Formboard, Series AA; the Minnesota Spatial Relations Test, Boards A and B; and the Minnesota Assembly Test, Sets I and II," he observed that deaf boys would do well to develop skills in such trades as "printing, linotyping, metal work, photoengraving, and woodwork," for "despite their limitations, the deaf are generally successful in vocational pursuits."[38]

Experiments have shown that when teachers are told that their students are "gifted" they often achieve far greater success with those students, even if the students have not been found to possess superior intellectual capacities at all. But the reverse is also true. Myklebust's text and others like it, dealing with the linguistic and psychological limitations of deaf people, were standard texts in teacher training programs. One can only imagine the effects of such negative input on teachers who would instruct deaf children. Researchers have since found that most of the tests used by Myklebust were either inappropriate or appropriate only if adequate communication between examiner and child could be guaranteed, through sign language or in writing. Nevertheless, for more than twenty years, Myklebust's findings were accepted without question.[39]

Carol Padden and Tom Humphries, two of today's foremost interpreters of deaf culture (both former students at Gallaudet), note that Myklebust's "authority" was "enough to establish the tone of official thought. For the next generation of those influential in deciding how deaf children in America would be taught, Helmer Myklebust's *Psychology of Deafness* set the standard."[40]

CHAPTER 2

. . . .

The education of the deaf was almost a family enterprise, and Gallaudet was the Daddy. Oralists were always treated with deference on the campus. The faculty, no matter how they truly felt, were almost obsequious in appeasing the oralists.

LOU FANT

From the time of its founding, Gallaudet College held out the promise of a continuation of the success that Thomas Hopkins Gallaudet had achieved by bringing sign language to America and using it to educate deaf students. But changes in the philosophy and practice of deaf education over the next hundred years took their toll; fewer and fewer deaf students attended college, and those who did were perceived by the hearing establishment that had gained control of their education to be suffering from a condition that encompassed "a wide variety of problems."[1]

For deaf people school has always been one of the few places where they can be together and experience the camaraderie of easy communication; even when they were forbidden to use their sign language in the classroom, deaf students used it among themselves — often in secret — in the dormitories and on the grounds. Lifelong friendships are made at these institutions. Often, when deaf people meet each other their first topic of conversation is which schools they have attended and when.

Gallaudet — the first and still the only liberal arts college in the world devoted exclusively to deaf students — was always held in high esteem among deaf people. It was the place where they could learn the history of their people, where they could gain knowledge of and pride in their culture, where they could be with others who viewed deafness as a condition, not as a handicap. So many Gallaudet graduates have gone on to make outstanding contributions in both the deaf and hearing societies that the school's alumni list reads like a *Who's Who* of deaf leaders in America. But the history of Gallaudet is inextricably woven into the history of the worldwide conflict between oralism and sign language. From the time of Edward Miner Gallaudet's presidency, this bitter debate has had a direct impact on the college. As oralism became the accepted mode of teaching and communication, it logically followed that the teachers and top administrators in schools for the deaf tended to be hearing advocates of oralism, depriving deaf people of the ability to represent themselves and their interests. Jerome Schein describes the conditions typical of American schools for the deaf in the 1940s and 1950s:

> Most deaf students [did] not have much contact with Deaf adults who could serve as role models. Their teachers, ad-

ministrators, and supporting educational personnel [were] most often normally hearing. Until the 1960s, the only Deaf employees students met in most schools were apt to work as janitors and houseparents. Deaf teachers, if the school employed any, were usually found only in the upper grades, where they would hold positions in vocational, not academic, departments.[2]

Although Gallaudet University's sole mission always was the education of deaf students, from its founding until 1988 all of its presidents and almost all of its board members were hearing, and very few of them knew sign language before arriving at the school. In 1957, for example, special arrangements had to be made to have a dean of the college attend board meetings to interpret for Boyce Williams, the only deaf member of the board.[3] (Williams, a Gallaudet graduate, was for many years the highest-ranking deaf person in the federal government.) In 1958 it was so rare for hearing faculty to know any sign language when hired that the president of the college, Dr. Leonard M. Elstad, explained to the House Appropriations Committee that "the salary scale at the college should be made attractive to offset the added difficulty of learning a new method of communication."[4] One must assume that the quality of instruction was adversely affected if the typical new faculty member had no knowledge of signing when hired to teach deaf students college-level material.

Those hearing presidents, board members, and faculty who had any training whatsoever in the teaching of deaf students had studied in graduate programs at "normal" schools of education where the benefits of oralism were espoused. Their training had focused on the teaching of speech and lipreading to deaf students. As a result, the attitudes of many administrators of Gallaudet University were similar to those in oral schools.

The results were predictable. In 1922 Percival Hall, the second president of the college, complained about the quality of students arriving at Gallaudet from residential schools:

> Lots of students are dropped the first or second year and only half who enter graduate. Admission is probationary. Students come who can't even find any given article in an encyclope-

dia. . . . Students were too dependent on their instructors; they were unable to think for themselves as well as unwilling. (Sympathy for the deaf child may make the child more and more dependent.) Many students who came to Gallaudet seemed unwilling or unable to make a sustained mental effort; the students lacked self-reliance; some students couldn't use the index of a textbook.[5]

President Hall did find comfort in an article written by a Gallaudet professor that appeared in *American Annals of the Deaf* in May of 1922. The subject was a printing course at Gallaudet: "Many students pick up a good education this way. Many of our young men who are good writers began in the print shop. It is especially good for the deaf boy, handicapped in language; constant spelling and the setting up of line after line of type have the tendency to fix in the mind correct sentence construction; the printer has a good chance of improving his English."[6]

Despite students' difficulties, surveys conducted by the college showed that Gallaudet graduates were leading productive and fulfilling lives. They owned their own homes and cars in equal proportion to hearing college graduates, and in 1931 Gallaudet graduates contributed $50,000 to honor the anniversary of the birth of Edward Miner Gallaudet. Typical hearing attitudes prevailed, however, at the presentation of the check by the alumni to the college. Secretary of the Interior Ray Wilbur noted that "it was an unusual circumstance for handicapped persons to be presenting their alma mater with a large sum of money from the earnings of their successful careers."[7]

Conditions and attitudes improved very little over the next forty years. In 1963 Irving S. Fusfeld, one of the former deans of the college, offered this assessment of the academic potential of deaf students: "Continued interest in academic study has little lure for deaf youth, who, even if they remain in school for the usual 12 or 13 years have a trade in hand with which to start their livelihood and perhaps a home of their own, and at an age when these are natural urges."[8]

Of course, oralism contributed to the belief that deaf people were deficient — less capable than hearing people. In 1958 the administrators and board members of Gallaudet saw fit to grant an honorary degree to Helmer Myklebust, the psychologist whose textbook *The Psychology of Deafness* had contributed so greatly to the perception among educators that deaf students were deficient.

In many cases, the students' signs were perceived as a kind of pantomime, accompanied by sounds and gestures, especially facial gestures, to which hearing people were unaccustomed and which they often found repugnant. Edward T. Hall, the anthropologist, recalls an example of these attitudes during the 1950s:

> At Gallaudet . . . I was asked to consult with psychologists who were attempting to solve a problem among the faculty. Hearing people there were disturbed by the fact that when the deaf signed, they also grimaced, which took the place of tone of voice. Hearing people found this distracting and tried to stop the deaf from this natural grimacing. It was an attempt to eliminate one of the basic building blocks of what is now known as deaf culture, but which hearing people saw as behavior which was chaotic and lacking in order.[9]

Arden Neisser, in *The Other Side of Silence*, describes Gallaudet in the early 1950s as "a sleepy educational backwater that was considered just about right for a handicapped population. . . . Gallaudet College, without attracting much attention, continued to do its job of teaching the seven or eight percent of deaf students who made it to college. Few faculty members had advanced degrees; there was no tradition of scholarship."[10]

Neisser was not exaggerating. In 1952 Dr. Leonard Elstad became Gallaudet's third president, and at that time he decided that the college should apply for accreditation to the Middle States Association of Colleges and Secondary Schools. The report of the association's evaluation committee, a 43-page indictment of the college, describes an institution straight out of Dickens, a Bleak House of higher education. While the report stresses that the faculty did its best to serve the students with an "eager and exuberant spirit," with "devotion to duty [and] zealous dedication in evidence," the rest of its findings were negative. It describes the purposes indicated in the Gallaudet catalogue as "hopes and promises, not goals which are susceptible of achievement at the present time, or ever for that matter, unless the zeal and devotion of the present staff are supplemented with tangible, substantial support in greater quantity than has been provided in the past."

The report notes that the Kendall School (the "lower" school and high school division of Gallaudet) excluded black children; that faculty with M.A.'s from Gallaudet had been granted higher rank than those who held Ph.D.'s from other institutions; that the school had no clear tenure policy, no director of admissions, and no institutional statutes or faculty handbook; and that the professional and clerical staff were insufficient.

More specifically, the report states that

- the multifarious teaching duties of the staff at Gallaudet are amazing — and indefensible;
- the practice of teaching in more than one subject-matter field generally prevails;
- the Professor of Chemistry . . . also functions as stock room clerk, custodian of supplies, etc.;
- a wider choice of courses is essential;
- [the language program] lacks adequate communications equipment;
- in Physics the equipment seems to be generally inferior, [and] the tendency is to regard Physics as a sort of Mathematics and to treat it as such;
- [Social Studies seems to be] a hodge-podge with many unrelated courses in diverse areas so far afield as Contemporary Affairs, Logic, Business Law, Comparative Religion, and Dramatics;
- office space is either totally lacking or inadequate (the Dean of Men interviews students at his home, for instance);
- [the library] is inadequate in the quantity and quality of its references and general texts and it is obviously inadequate in space;
- the fifth-year program designed as a graduate program for hearing persons to be trained as teachers of the deaf has a loosely constructed admission policy — in the group that has been admitted for the school year 1952–53, the academic ability, according to previous college training, ranges from a 1.0 grade point average to 2.7;
- some of the teachers in the Kendall School without degrees

are serving as critics for the students who are possessors of
Bachelor's degrees;

• Kendall School [given its mission to train teachers] should
include courses in child development [because there]
appears to be a decided lack of understanding that teachers
should know about normal physical, emotional, social and
mental growth before they become specialists to work with
and understand children with a physical impairment;

• the physical education offerings are meager without courses
in anatomy and kinesiology, but yet . . . a student, taking
three years of basic physical education activities plus two
courses, one first aid and the other community hygiene,
could qualify to teach physical education in a State School
for the Deaf;

• no one on the staff, except perhaps the Dean and the
President, is acquainted with the [organizational] charts
. . . it is not surprising to find some discrepancies between
the chart and the actual practice;

• attendance at Board meetings and interest in the College by
some members is "only fair," and this fact assumes a
greater significance when one considers that the Board is
not large to begin with."[11]

Shocked at the severity of the criticism leveled at the college,
President Elstad ordered Dean Fusfeld to study the report.
Fusfeld was able to quibble with some points, but concluded:
"There can be little question that many of the observations
reflecting critical conditions are valid."[12]

As a result, Elstad and Fusfeld decided that they needed,
among other things, a "curriculum expert." They found George
Ernst Detmold, a Cornell Ph.D. with a certificate in administration from Teachers College of Columbia University. Detmold
had absolutely no experience with a deaf population, but since
that had never been a prerequisite for employment at Gallaudet
University, he was hired as Dean of Instruction, anyway. His
real job, however, was "to get the place accredited."[13]

It was the beginning of a new era at Gallaudet. Detmold had
no prior loyalties to anyone at the school; he had no precon-
ceived notions about deaf people; and he was given free rein to
hire new faculty, change and improve the curriculum, and insti-

tute new policies. His task was enormous. Despite having read the report of the Middle States Association and served on evaluation committees that had denied accreditation to other universities, he was unprepared for what he found. When he arrived at Gallaudet in September of 1952, he discovered that the college,

> though small, was the headquarters of a large political enterprise, called by those in it "the profession." Actually, it meant the control of the state residential schools for the deaf, where more than half of deaf children were educated. Superintendents of these schools were appointed by the state legislators and most went directly to them for funding. But very few got this appointment without the recommendation of the president of Gallaudet College. The Gallaudet M.A. in the education of the deaf was the road (for men only) to a principalship and later superintendency. . . . Some men, already "trained teachers of the deaf," came to Gallaudet for a repeat, in order to get its imprimatur.
>
> When I arrived in 1952, the Department of Education was still being called the Normal Department. People there thought that "normal" meant not deaf. Deaf people were not admitted. It was customary to say of a superintendent who had the Gallaudet M.A. that "he was Normal in '38."
>
> [President] Elstad . . . beefed up the faculty by hiring its second Ph.D., but [Dean] Fusfeld, then and later, advised against trying for accreditation because the college was too "special." Many agreed with him, both faculty and alumni, arguing that standards applied to other colleges should not apply to Gallaudet.[14]

President Elstad gave Detmold five years to get the college accredited, arguing that if it couldn't be accredited in that amount of time, "it shouldn't exist." Detmold remembers that Elstad took "a lot of flak from his friends the superintendents [of residential deaf schools] who told him he was crazy to think that deaf people could ever be liberally educated."

Detmold discovered that the faculty at Gallaudet at the time was an even mix of hearing and deaf and was "fairly enthusiastic" but utterly without direction: one professor "taught public speaking and anything else that he felt like," another "taught physical education and anything else for which no other teacher could be found, on the theory that a 'trained teacher of the deaf' can teach deaf students anything."

Curious about a popular course in public speaking, Detmold noticed that every time he passed the classroom "all the students were asleep, with their heads on their desks. 'What's going on?' I asked the professor, a highly respected deaf man on campus. He was offended. Didn't I know that deaf people used their eyes more than hearing people? Therefore, in his class he insisted that they rest their eyes."

Detmold found such overindulgent practices and attitudes throughout the deaf education system:

> To begin with, [the students'] secondary education . . . was almost nonexistent. That we admitted only the top 10 percent of them is evidence that they were among the brightest of their generation. Nonetheless, almost all of them were admitted to the preparatory class, where they had a year of math (algebra and geometry) and English composition. If they survived that, they became undergraduates, where a poor repast awaited them. The most advanced course offered in math was an introduction to calculus, ordinarily given in high school. [One professor] offered acceptable courses in chemistry, but [another] merely fiddled around in elementary biology. He believed that the deaf couldn't read but liked to look at pictures, so he ordered *Life* magazine for them instead of a textbook. There was no physics. . . . English and American history were taught in the curious mechanical way in which teachers were supposed to teach language to the deaf. The sociology course was the kind that you would find in high school. There was no economics.

Detmold soon realized that the watered-down curriculum was a direct result of common attitudes toward deaf people: expectations for deaf graduates, he remembers, were "extremely limited." Most of the male students would become dormitory supervisors in the residential high schools that they had attended, "hoping at some time to be allowed to teach." Others would learn printing and go directly after college to the Government Printing Office or teach printing in vocational schools for the deaf. The girls would often return to their residential schools as well, to teach sewing and cooking.

Detmold recalls that "there was no idea that Gallaudet graduates could ever compete in the big world outside with the graduates of other colleges." The professor who had taught Detmold signing told him that deaf students had "frozen minds." Another professor, who referred to deaf students as "the deef," explained to Detmold that they "can't think in the abstract." Detmold quickly determined that he would have to change such attitudes among the faculty, the administration, and the students.

Detmold remembers the conditions that were accepted as "normal" at the time of his arrival: there was no registrar (the president's secretary kept the student records); the dean of the college was also the admissions officer, preparing the entrance examinations, sending them to high schools, and grading them when they were returned. Meetings were not held on a regular basis; the most important meeting took place at the beginning of each year to plan course offerings and schedules. There was no bookstore; the business office placed teachers' orders and distributed the books when they arrived, often when the semester was half over. No college catalog was printed the year Detmold arrived; instead, the catalog from the year before was reprinted. The school had no dean of students, no counseling service. The president's personal doctor also served as the college physician. There were no faculty offices; teachers who lived off campus often used their cars as offices.

What upset Detmold most, however, was the inbreeding on the Board of Directors: "They were all local men. Executive committee meetings were frequently held before or after the regular Rotary lunch. Practically all members of the board eventually received an honorary doctorate. So did many of the superintendents. One of my least favorable duties was the writing of citations for these honorary degrees."[15]

In 1955 Detmold asked one of his oldest and best friends, Bill Stokoe, to accept a teaching position in Gallaudet's English Department. Detmold still remembers the pleasure he felt when Stokoe accepted his offer; President Elstad had told him that he "would never get real Ph.D.'s to come to Gallaudet."[16] But Detmold's greatest pleasure stemmed from the fact that his best friend would join him at Gallaudet.

George Detmold and Bill Stokoe had met at Cornell University in 1937, when Detmold was a junior and Stokoe a sophomore. They became acquainted in the fencing room, where Detmold was assistant coach. Fencing became one of the many interests they would share during their long friendship (which continues to the present day); they also enjoyed sailing, hunting, shooting, tennis, drama, and literature. Both men remained at Cornell for graduate work: Detmold wrote his master's thesis on Shakespeare's *Coriolanus* and received his Ph.D. in literature after completing a dissertation on the origins of drama. Stokoe's dissertation was entitled "The Work of the Redactors of *Sir Launfal, Richard Coeur de Lion* and *Sir Degaré.*"

These topics were better preparation for a career at Gallaudet than one might think. Detmold directed plays with deaf actors at Gallaudet; it was he who encouraged Gil Eastman, the author of *Sign Me Alice*, to complete graduate work at the Catholic University of America and to return to Gallaudet to chair the Theater Arts Department. Stokoe's *lack* of formal linguistic training (with the exception of two undergraduate courses) may have helped him see language in an unconventional way, and his translations of Old and Middle English poetry and literature certainly contributed to his appreciation of the variety and richness of languages and his understanding of the changes they undergo.

Before coming to Gallaudet both Detmold and Stokoe had had limited but positive experience with deaf people. Near the farm where Stokoe grew up lived a deaf blacksmith. Stokoe remembers that the blacksmith "had a pad right near the doorway into his forge where you could write down what you wanted, but in most cases he would just take a look at what you carried in and know what had to be done to fix it. . . . He did beautiful work, and he was very independent — you knew that he observed everything that went on in the village."[17] Detmold had known a deaf man in Aurora, New York, who umpired at local softball games. "He was a good umpire because nobody could argue with him," Detmold recalls.[18]

In neither case did deafness preclude a full, satisfying, productive life of involvement in the larger society. For Detmold and Stokoe, knowing these men suggested a rather different view from the one usually inculcated into hearing teachers and transmitted through the education process to many deaf people: that deafness leads to "an inability to . . . know the world directly . . . and [that deaf people] are condemned to a life lacking the depth of meaning that sound makes available to hearing people."[19]

After Cornell, George Detmold enlisted in the army — it was 1942. His military service was not typical, however; he was sent to Yale to learn Chinese and then served in the X Force of the Chinese Training and Combat Command.

Bill Stokoe hoped to enlist as well, and he enrolled in Cornell's ROTC program. His grades had always been excellent, but he had to work hard to win a Boldt Scholarship to supplement other scholarships he had won. His family owned a farm, but his parents "felt the strain of tuition" — they were once forced to sell a prize heifer to keep him in college. Stokoe's studies, along with his job scrubbing pots to earn free meals and his commitment to the fencing team, exhausted him. In the summer of 1940, while training at ROTC camp in Plattsburgh, Stokoe had a nervous breakdown. He spent several days in the camp hospital, "incoherent most of the time" but aware of "the madness of the place." He was sent home and saw a psychiatrist, who diagnosed him as manic-depressive and prescribed medication. He didn't want to leave the house or see anyone but family for several weeks. He was classified 4F as a result of his illness and "took a whole year off to get back inside myself." When he returned to Cornell in the fall of 1941, he made Phi Beta Kappa, again received the Boldt Scholarship, and was elected co-captain of the fencing team. His illness was relatively brief and never recurred, but even today, forty years later, Stokoe finds it painful to explain "how I sat out the war."[20]

Soon after recovering, Bill Stokoe met Ruth Palmeter, a fellow student at Cornell. He remembers the circumstances of their first meeting, their first conversation, their first date, what she wore, where they went. She was the perfect antidote to the breakdown he had suffered. He proposed marriage on their third date, and she accepted. They were married in November of 1942, despite his mother's misgivings that perhaps Ruth was a bit of "the party girl."

Less than a month after they were married, Ruth proved her strength and stability as she helped her new husband endure the grief of losing his only sibling. Bill and his brother Jim, who was two years younger, had been inseparable in childhood: hunting, hiking, fishing, working long hours on the family farm in Stafford, New York, attending the same elementary and high schools. In December 1942, Jim was found alone at the farm, dead from a bullet wound in the head. Although the coroner ruled the death a suicide, Bill Stokoe remains convinced that it was an accident. "There was no investigation other than the deputy sheriff's, and Jim was preparing for a hunt, hence the gun, and looking forward to getting married in a couple of weeks." Jim's death was the worst hurdle Bill Stokoe had ever had to face, and George Detmold remembers that for many years Bill spoke about his brother as if he were still alive. Stokoe believes that his brother's death changed him; he feels that he "absorbed" some of his brother's qualities, that he was "softened" and "made more human."[21]

After the death of Jim Stokoe, Bill and Ruth Stokoe were needed to help run the family farm because Bill's parents both held full-time teaching positions. Ruth Stokoe "became a farmer's wife," raising chickens, cooking, and baking. But both she and Bill Stokoe knew that farm life wasn't for them. Stokoe applied for and was accepted into graduate school at Cornell in 1943.

When George Detmold was discharged from the army in late 1945, he returned to Cornell to teach (and to coach fencing), and he and Stokoe resumed their friendship. Soon after, in 1946, Stokoe was offered an assistant professorship at Wells College, a women's school on Cayuga Lake at Aurora, not far from Cornell. Stokoe chose the position over one offered by Yale. In 1947, on the basis of a recommendation from Stokoe, then chair of the English Department, Detmold was also offered a position at Wells. He and Stokoe continued to work and socialize together for the next four years.

Their training at Cornell had an enormous impact on their

teaching philosophies. There, they had formed the conviction that every student is worthy of unlimited respect and possesses high potential in keeping with his or her individual talents, individual learning skills, and individual goals. They developed their pedagogical views not in educational psychology and methodology classes but under the tutelage of Henry Myers, Detmold's graduate advisor and one of Stokoe's graduate professors. Detmold describes the effect of Myers's book, *Are Men Equal? An Inquiry into the Meaning of American Democracy*, on him and Bill Stokoe:

> Myers argues that each man (please accept the term generically) is to himself the center of an infinite universe; that each of us is to himself, therefore, of infinite worth; and that — since things equal to the same thing are equal to each other — men are indeed, in their infinite worth, equal. He develops this theme as it comes and goes throughout American history and literature, showing how we suffer when we forget it. Henry's book certainly guided me, especially at Gallaudet, and it guided Bill as well. He often refers to it.[22]

This humanistic view is in stark contrast to the philosophy of deaf education that prevailed when Detmold and Stokoe began teaching. The two men had never heard of Helmer Myklebust; they had never been instructed in the anatomy and physiology of the ear; they hadn't learned how to administer hearing tests and distinguish among hearing aids; they hadn't learned about the various types of audiometry as had their "properly trained" counterparts.

This is not to say that Bill Stokoe wasn't afraid of the move he was about to make. In 1955, although jobs in academia were scarce, and although his contract had not been renewed at Wells College, his credentials were excellent, and he probably could have found another position quickly. He recalls the difficulty of arriving at a decision:

> Would working again with George Detmold outweigh having to recast my lecturing and class meeting and conference style into a manual mode? Could I function where my voice would simply not be heard?

The Modern Language Association had published two parts of my three-part dissertation on Middle English romances translated from Old French. Even better, the *University of Toronto Quarterly* had published in 1952 my interpretation of a major part of *The Canterbury Tales*. Still better — if the decision was to go on in the mainstream of English teaching and making contributions to mainstream scholarship — I had been asked to present a paper at the MLA annual meeting on the work of Gavin Douglas, the fifteenth-century Chaucerian and main focus of my sabbatical studies. As the time for deciding shortened, I had a paper accepted for publication by *Speculum*, the journal of medieval studies.[23]

Stokoe's strong admiration for George Detmold and their long-term friendship were important factors in his decision to accept the position at Gallaudet. The two men enjoyed each other's company and admired each other's intellect. Detmold was Bill Stokoe's most trusted friend, particularly after the death of Jim Stokoe. These two humanists — one a Shakespearean scholar with a passion for theater, the other an expert on Chaucer and other Old and Middle English authors — would share the same camaraderie at Gallaudet that they had shared at Cornell and Wells.

But while they had left Cornell and Wells pretty much the same as they had found them, they brought irrevocable change to Gallaudet University, its deaf faculty and students, and deaf people around the world, including many who might never know of their existence. When George Detmold arrived at Gallaudet in 1952 and when Bill Stokoe arrived three years later, they believed that deaf people were no different from hearing people in their worth as individuals. Like everyone else, deaf people were entitled to justice — the kind of justice Walt Whitman described when he wrote: "It is immutable — it does not depend on majorities."[24]

It was William Stokoe's observations and discoveries that led to the recognition of American Sign Language as a complete and sophisticated language system, and it was Stokoe who encouraged both deaf and hearing researchers to develop the field of sign language linguistics. But it was George Detmold who fought with the Gallaudet administration, with the faculty, even with the students, to give Stokoe the time, space, and funding necessary for his work.

Thirty-five years later, the work of William Stokoe came to fruition in one of the most dramatic demands for justice and equality that deaf people in this country have ever asserted. When Gallaudet's first deaf president, I. King Jordan, declared that "deaf people can do anything but hear," he expressed a truth that was new to many people in the United States and the world. Bill Stokoe and George Detmold had recognized that truth for most of their lives.

CHAPTER 3

. . . .

There was no linguistic attention, no scientific attention, given to Sign until the late 1950s when William Stokoe . . . found his way to Gallaudet College. Stokoe thought he had come to teach Chaucer to the deaf; but he very soon perceived that he had been thrown, by good fortune or chance, into one of the world's most extraordinary linguistic environments.

OLIVER SACKS *Seeing Voices*

Bill Stokoe was not traveling light when he moved from Wells College in Aurora, New York, to Gallaudet University in Washington, D.C. He was thirty-six years old, and his academic credentials were excellent. But neither he nor Ruth Stokoe had come from wealthy families, and they now had two children to support: Helen Marie Stokoe, born in 1947, and James Stafford Stokoe (named after Bill's brother), born in 1951.

George Detmold still remembers the move. Bill and Ruth Stokoe drove with the two children in their station wagon; Detmold followed in a rented truck containing all of the Stokoes' possessions.

The Stokoes' first rented house was infested with water beetles; so was the second one. But they were soon able to buy a small, comfortable house in Silver Spring, Maryland — about a twenty-minute commute from Gallaudet. Their living arrangement was typical in 1955: a house in the suburbs, a mother who stayed home with the children and did volunteer work, a father who left for work each morning and returned each evening with a briefcase filled with paperwork to find dinner on the table. But Stokoe was anything but typical. Although he wore the requisite suit, tie, and vest to classes, he arrived on a motorcycle. People at Gallaudet still tell jokes about his passion for playing the bagpipes. Barbara Kannapell, a student at Gallaudet at the time, was amused by Bill Stokoe's logic in practicing the pipes on campus rather than at home: the students wouldn't have to hear him.[1]

At Gallaudet, Stokoe pursued the literary themes that had interested him at Cornell and Wells. He continued to publish articles: "The Double Problem of Sir Degaré" in 1955 and "On Ohthere's *Steorbord*" in 1957. As a young professor, Stokoe was well aware of the "publish or perish" mentality that existed in academia, so he was particularly pleased at being published in prestigious literary journals. But his writing was inspired more by a passion for research — an obsession, some would say — than by the need to be published. At Wells he had spent a large part of his year-long sabbatical in Scotland solving the problem of "the reading of a single word in King Alfred's translation of Orosius's *Geography* into the Anglo Saxon of Wessex."[2] (He still found time, however, to practice his bagpipes on the Scottish shore.)

Within days of his arrival at Gallaudet, Bill Stokoe was introduced to his next research project — one that would last for the rest of his life. He began lessons in what everyone then called "the sign language." These lessons marked the beginning of a lifetime of learning, analyzing, and promoting a language that was still considered by many to be a convenient but inadequate system of communication — almost a necessary evil.

Although the oralists had determined that all signing should be banned in favor of speech and lipreading, sign language had never been completely eliminated in the United States. Many deaf people signed among themselves, of course, but signing was also tolerated in deaf schools and used by staff, not only with children who had been labeled "oral failures" but in various other contexts as well. In an essay outlining the history of the use of American Sign Language, Mimi WheiPing Lou explains:

> Not surprisingly, religious groups and clergy had already recognized the difficulty of communicating with the Deaf through oral-only methods. Thus, in the 1900s clergy began learning sign language, and religious groups began to go on record as supporting the use of sign language. An interesting situation developed at some schools . . . where teachers were required to use the oral method but clergy were permitted to use sign language. By the 1940s an increasing number of seminaries were offering sign language to those who would be working with the Deaf community. . . . When communication was a means to some other end, . . . then sign language was accepted and used. When a particular communication system — that is, English — was itself the goal of education, then manual approaches were avoided, if not completely banned."[3]

However, the "signing" that hearing instructors used to teach deaf students in these schools was actually a system of manually coded English. Lou Fant, a Gallaudet professor whose parents were deaf, explains that during the 1950s

> There were few classes in sign language. Gallaudet had a class for those graduate students studying to become school teachers. . . . A few schools for deaf children had "survival" classes

for new teachers to help save them from being completely lost, and a few classes thrived in church basements. None of these classes taught ASL [American Sign Language], but rather taught a system of manually coded English.

Like most children of deaf parents, I grew up with no conscious awareness that ASL was a language. I thought of ASL as an ungrammatical parody of English.[4]

Bill Stokoe was introduced to signing for the first time in one of those "survival" classes at Gallaudet. In the morning he studied with Elizabeth Benson, dean of women and the daughter of deaf parents; his afternoon teacher was Dick Phillips, a deaf professor who was also dean of men.

Stokoe quickly realized that the signs he was being taught were very different from the signs his students were using, and he realized, as well, the difficulty his students would have in understanding his halting, stiff signing. Elizabeth Benson, he recalls, was "teaching sign translation of English, or a literal, sign-for-word translation of English." In addition, she insisted that he and the other new professors "spend a lot of time just learning to fingerspell" because she was "very sure that the teachers should comport themselves in language as well as behavior as befitted teachers in an institution of higher education." This was the first of many times Stokoe was told that the signs the students used among themselves were "inappropriate" for "formal" situations.

> I realized immediately that the deaf students on campus were not using signs the same way that we were. Even though the signs represented the same word, the students performed them differently. We were to avoid slang, as Elizabeth Benson called it — in other words, we were to avoid the language the students used.
>
> Some years later, I observed Miss Benson giving a class in communication to health workers, nurses, and social workers, people who would not be teaching deaf students formally in classes but working with deaf people. She was teaching them facial expression. She told them to use pantomime or whatever they needed to communicate. It was just the opposite, really, of what she taught us to do in classes.

I received about three weeks of that kind of instruction, and then we were on our own in the classes. We were supposed to speak and sign at the same time. We didn't have interpreters. We proceeded slowly and roughly, and the students were often tolerant enough to help us when we needed a sign, or to stop us when what we had done wasn't clear. It must have been horrible, but we got through it somehow. I wondered whether I really ever would learn to interact thoroughly enough with the students to be of any positive value.[5]

Before he taught his first class at Gallaudet, Stokoe realized that he wasn't going to achieve his goals of teaching his students to read and write English well and to develop an appreciation of English literature unless he learned their language. He recalls two experiences, both involving deaf professors, that helped him to understand the crucial relationship between communication and teaching. The first was with Carl G. Croneberg, an English professor with whom Stokoe would later collaborate on *A Dictionary of American Sign Language on Linguistic Principles.*

Carl had a student come in with a paper that contained the word "backlog," and the student didn't know what the word meant; he had never encountered it before. Carl started to explain it to him in signing and in fingerspelling, and the student suddenly signed "understand." The student then made a sign which, literally translated, meant "have behind." Once the student had grasped the idea, he almost automatically came out with its expression in ASL.

It was in the classroom of another deaf professor, Robert Panara, that Stokoe first saw sign language used effectively to teach. The experience, he recalls, was

a real eye-opener. . . . [Panara] was the best lecturer in sign language going. During the class, he was discussing the novel *Wuthering Heights.* What was fascinating about his performance was that he used one hand to talk about Heathcliff, spelling the name at first with that hand, then just using the letter *H* on that hand. Then he used the other hand to represent the name Cathy, again fingerspelled at first. That *C* became the hand for talking about, signing about, what

Cathy did. Not only could he separate the two characters in that manner rather than using "he" and "she" as one would in English discourse — he could sign interaction between them. Instead of calling attention to one side of his body or the other, where his hand was forming the initial, he could move them in signs and show the relationship between the two characters — side to side.

It struck me at that time that here was an absolutely fascinating way of conducting a course in English literature, and it was something that I'd have to learn to do after some kind of fashion if I wanted to succeed in teaching my subject.[6]

Without realizing it, without being told to, Stokoe was doing what Thomas Hopkins Gallaudet had done more than 150 years ago: Gallaudet had gone to deaf people to ask them to teach him their language before he would dare to try to teach them his. "Right from the start," Stokoe recalls, "I'd ask the deaf members of the department to help me. I'd ask them what the sign was for this word, how they handled this, that, and the other thing. They were most helpful to me."[7]

But Stokoe's signing was atrocious. It wasn't that he couldn't remember the signs; his facility with languages (he had studied Latin, Greek, French, and German at Cornell), his enthusiasm, and his excellent memory served him well in that regard. But signing, which requires a certain amount of manual dexterity and skill, is easier for some people than others, and Stokoe never attained the fluidity of motion he desired. Carl Croneberg, Stokoe's deaf colleague in the English department, explains: "There are . . . a small number of hearing people who use the sign language fluently. Most of these are teachers of the deaf or children of deaf parents. But as a rule, hearing people having some knowledge of the language of signs cannot be classified as native signers. For any given person, a certain frequency of inter-group contact is necessary for acquiring the language of this group; the extent to which a person can be called a native speaker varies with the frequency of this contact."[8]

I. King Jordan, the first deaf president of Gallaudet University and a good friend of Stokoe's, notes that although "Bill has a tremendously large sign vocabulary," his signing is "laborious.

His manual dexterity or fluency or smoothness in signing really leaves something to be desired. He's easy to understand for a person like me [Jordan lost his hearing as a young adult]. I honestly don't know for a person who is not as fluent in English as I. I don't know how easy Bill would be to understand. He knows all the signs and he doesn't have to look for the right sign. He just doesn't sign easily. He seems to have to work to do it."[9]

It seems ironic: the man many describe as "the Father of American Sign Language" doesn't sign very well. Perhaps Stokoe's difficulty in using the language, his inability to take it for granted as simply a method of communication, and his need to look at it carefully were responsible, in part, for his discoveries. It took an "outsider" to see what had been there all along.

But it took a special kind of outsider: one who believed that "the study of sign language could free . . . a teacher from the fear and ignorance that equate all knowledge and thought with a single language."[10] Carol Padden says in describing Bill Stokoe's limitations as a signer, "His fingerspelling is usually unreadable, but I'd rather have novelty and intelligence with bad fingerspelling than oppression and intolerance disguised in great signing skills."[11]

Stokoe has his own theory about his entry into sign language research. He once heard his son, Jim, reading a story to his grandson, Nathaniel. When the boy in the story declared that he wanted to be a veterinarian who talked to animals, Dr. Dolittle replied: "First, I've got to ask you, are you a noticing person?" And that, Stokoe says, is as good a description of his philosophy as any:

A hearing person entering into a deaf environment must notice what is going on. I think that one of the first things I noticed was that the deaf people on campus didn't communicate the way we were being told we should communicate in our classrooms.

Then you've got to notice what the students can do. Don't read the literature on deaf education because that will tell you what they can't do. That will tell you about the hearing loss, the mental deficit, the language deficit, the years of retardation in school achievement, and all the rest of it. Ignore all that and notice the students.

Find out what they *can* do and want to do and encourage them to want to do more. Show them how to do it. Don't tell them but show them on the board or on paper or with signs — if you can sign — and give them a chance to try it. Be generous with praise when they do it right, and be as careful as can be when you are criticizing the mistakes they make. Remember how brilliant they must be to have gotten where they are, to have made it to an institution of higher education under the circumstances which existed for them.[12]

This is not to say that Stokoe's early experiences at Gallaudet were easy. Initially, the students resented Stokoe's arrival. Gil Eastman, who was a Gallaudet student at the time, recalls the resistance he and the other students felt toward Detmold's reforms and their suspicion that Stokoe had been hired simply because he was "Detmold's friend." Eastman, who eventually headed the Theater Arts Department and became one of the best known deaf actors and playwrights in the country, recalls that the students complained about the new curriculum primarily because of their reluctance to change:

> The students' argument [against] the new curriculum lasted through the rest of the academic year. In the fall of 1953, the Gallaudet freshmen invaded Dr. Detmold's office to protest his drastic changes in [the] curriculum. We were lost in chaos. We had to take brand new courses that had never been offered before. We said that it was not fair to the past students. It was a tough program. We often planned a boycott [but that] never happened. Several months later we got used to the changes but we still did not like Detmold's transformation.[13]

In October of 1955, when Bill Stokoe's arrival was announced in the *Buff and Blue* (the school newspaper), the students held his friendship with Detmold against him. Eastman remembers a group of students complaining: "Not fair! Why did he hire his own friend? I am not going to take a course under him. I heard he is a tough teacher. I prefer deaf instructors in the English Department. Stokoe just learned sign language. Why should I waste my time watching him sign slowly and stiffly?"[14]

Some of the Gallaudet faculty members were also put off by Stokoe. His friendship with Detmold was a constant source of gossip on campus. Detmold remembers that "other faculty complained that I was spending all my time with Bill, and doubtless showing him favors that they did not receive. 'The captain dines alone.' I know this, but was resolved not to run that lonely a ship, and I tried to keep my friendship with Bill in balance with my responsibilities to everyone else."[15]

Detmold's attempts to achieve a delicate balance were not entirely successful. Bob Panara, the deaf professor whose teaching and signing skills Stokoe so admired, recalls that Detmold and Stokoe "flaunted" their friendship:

> George Detmold and William Stokoe made it a practice to go out to lunch practically every day after a round of tennis. They were that close. And they were closemouthed about many things. At that time, Gallaudet was trying to get accredited and Detmold brought in many Ph.D.'s to teach, some of whom were in my department. We had to add many new courses in order to establish a bona fide English major: "Beowulf," "Chaucer," "Victorian Literature," "The Romantic Period," and so forth. Who do you think was given the responsibility to teach these courses? Yours truly, as I had the signing skills and had been attending Catholic University for my Ph.D. Yet George Detmold appointed William Stokoe as chairman of the department — the position that I had held until he arrived. Furthermore, William Stokoe . . . was not very competent, as he lacked sign communication skills.[16]

The man whose work empowered deaf people by demonstrating that they possessed a language and culture of their own, the man whose work helped spark the Deaf President Now movement, the man whose work ultimately expanded educational and employment opportunities for deaf people, took a job away from a deaf man. Bob Panara explains the circumstances at the time and the reaction of other deaf faculty to Stokoe's appointment:

> Sure, lots of my friends and colleagues talked about the "unfairness" of the fact that I was replaced as chairman by Bill Stokoe. However, this was 1956, and if you understand deaf education in the schools and at Gallaudet during that era and before, you will understand that we were much like the Negro at that time; we felt "lucky" to have our jobs as teachers of the deaf in the state schools, more so at Gallaudet, and we were all resigned to the fact that deaf education was controlled by "the hearing world." Call us "Deaf Uncle Toms," but you have to have been there in that day and age, in our shoes, to understand.[17]

Detmold earned even more enemies among the deaf students on campus over the case of Ted Hughes, a deaf professor who had directed the theater program at Gallaudet for years and was a particularly popular figure on campus. Detmold knew what he had to do to get the college accredited, and in the process he decided to have Ted Hughes stop teaching the drama course. Bob Panara remembers that Detmold assessed Hughes's course as "equal to a high school curriculum." (Judging from the Middle States Association report and Detmold's observations, this may have been a diplomatic understatement. It was Hughes who had ordered *Life* magazine as a text and permitted his students to put their heads on their desks to rest their eyes.) According to Panara, Detmold's actions broke Hughes's heart. "He never again attended any Gallaudet plays," Panara recalls. "About three years later, when the senior class finally got him on stage again to accept the honor of having the yearbook dedicated to him, he suffered a heart attack and died right on stage. About a year later, George Detmold took over as director of the Gallaudet theater since he had a Ph.D. in drama."[18]

It is easy to imagine the resentment such incidents must have engendered. In retrospect, Detmold's desire to spend time with Bill Stokoe, his oldest and best friend, seems reasonable enough, and the changes he made in the faculty and administration were essential in order to obtain accreditation. However,

Detmold and Stokoe must have sensed that their actions were alienating, even offensive, to the deaf faculty and students.

Perhaps their behavior can be understood, in part, as that of members of a minority culture: at Gallaudet, Stokoe and Detmold found themselves in the position that deaf people often occupy in the hearing world. Detmold and Stokoe were the outsiders — they were hearing and had no family ties to deaf people; they arrived on campus with no sign language skills and no knowledge of deaf culture, attitudes, or customs. Even if they had scrupulously avoided any appearance of cronyism, one wonders how quickly they would have been accepted at the one institution of higher education in the nation where deaf people were in the majority.

As Carol Padden and Tom Humphries have pointed out in *Deaf in America*, "Deaf people must live almost entirely within the world of others. This peculiar social condition leads to a longing to live lives designed by themselves rather than those imposed by others."[19] Gallaudet was one of the few institutions in the nation where deaf people could hope to satisfy this longing — and now George Detmold, a hearing outsider, was "imposing" new rules on the students and taking jobs and responsibilities away from deaf people in the process.

Detmold's reforms also earned him praise, however. Jerome Schein, who joined the Gallaudet faculty in 1960, notes that Detmold "moved Gallaudet from an unaccredited backwater to a fully accredited college — something for which he has never received the credit he so richly deserves."[20]

I. King Jordan also praises Detmold's reforms. Detmold, he explains, was "the man behind the man. President Elstad gets credit for all the growth that Gallaudet went through and for the fact that Gallaudet was accredited and really became a college during his presidency. But it must be remembered that he hired George Detmold to do that."[21]

Stokoe's friendship with Detmold wasn't the only cause of difficulty during his first year at Gallaudet. The subject Stokoe taught was exceedingly difficult and inaccessible. His passion for medieval literature and languages made him seem arrogant and pedantic to the other faculty and students.

Stokoe remembers how surprised and pleased he was that his deaf students

> could pronounce Middle English better than my hearing students had. That seemed a little surprising at first since they couldn't hear, but when you stop to think about it, it's quite logical. They never did assume that what they were looking at could be read off the page like the language they spoke. They realized from long experience that when they saw something on the page they had to learn the code for turning those letter sequences into sounds. With them, as with all my students in Chaucer, I would show them how Middle English was supposed to sound, what the letter combination stood for in the way of vocal production, so my Gallaudet students could read a short passage of Middle English with better pronunciation than my hearing students had.[22]

As always, Stokoe was quick to recognize the intelligence and adaptability of his students, and he respected them enough to realize that Chaucer's work would be as accessible to them as to hearing students. But what, one wonders, did he think a class of deaf students would gain from reading Chaucer aloud to each other?

Bob Panara remembers that "except for the few students who were postlingually deaf [had lost their hearing after acquiring language] and highly literate, none of them could fathom what Bill was trying to get across when he taught Chaucer."[23]

Robbin Battison, one of Bill Stokoe's closest colleagues during the early 1970s, when they worked together in the Linguistics Research Lab, explains what he calls the "characteristics," rather than "shortcomings," of Bill Stokoe as an instructor:

> I think his wit and humor went above the heads of many people around him at Gallaudet, certainly above the heads of the deaf people around him, because most of his wit was very English-centered and wasn't easily translated into sign language, although he vainly tried to do so. I guess I'd use the word "starchy" to describe how many people perceived him.

He was perceived by many students and colleagues as being kind of boring and old-fashioned, even though of course he wasn't. He just came from a different culture; he was born in a different age. He was sometimes unnecessarily academic, but that may come from his being educated in the classics.

Bill was not essentially a very good teacher. He couldn't inspire people very easily. He tended to complicate his message, whether he wrote it or whether he spoke it. He tended to burden his message with complicated metaphors and literary allusions, and so the message had a hard time getting out. I think in some ways he worked against himself.[24]

But if Stokoe did find it difficult to get through to his students, this probably had as much to do with his training and the culture of the times as with his personality and teaching style. Up until the time he arrived at Gallaudet, he had taught students who had been speaking, hearing, reading, and writing English all of their lives.

Stokoe arrived at Gallaudet utterly unprepared for the poor reading and writing skills of his students. He never blamed them for their shortcomings; he realized it was his responsibility — and that of the other teachers — to help the students to develop the skills and strategies necessary to improve their reading and writing.

As chair of the English Department, Stokoe inherited a system that entitled each student enrolled in a class to spend half an hour a week alone with the professor — much to the chagrin of some faculty who, in Stokoe's words, "preferred to lecture once and get it over with." Stokoe approved of this individual tutorial system because it enabled him to interact with his students, get to know them better, and most important, help them achieve the academic goals he was convinced they were capable of — with the proper guidance and instruction.

Those individual sessions revealed to me precisely where the students needed help. When I read their papers through, if there was a part that I couldn't understand, I could simply ask the student questions, and he or she would usually respond, "Oh, I forgot that," and put in what was missing or insert the connecting idea.

There were teachers, however, who simply did not consider the students' needs or interests. Instead they complained that the college shouldn't have let the students in because they didn't know how to write an English sentence, or because their grammar was inadequate, or that they didn't seem to have any motivation.[25]

Stokoe was learning as he went along. As he compared the way the deaf professors taught with the approach of many hearing professors who had been "trained" to teach deaf students, he became convinced that the trained teachers not only lacked solutions but were the cause of many of the problems. The trained teachers of the deaf were (and still are), he says, afflicted with the wider

> American cultural complex: "If it ain't English, it ain't language." They and their graduate school teachers [are] hard to convince that another language is in the picture, even when they live in Florida or Texas and the other language is Spanish. After all, they can argue that these people are in this country now and [that] what their education has to give them is the ability to get along in correct English.
>
> To convince them that a language without sounds is a language is harder by several orders of magnitude. They have spent expensive credit hours learning the anatomy of the outer, middle, and inner ear, and of the organs of speech, not to mention the etiology and so forth of hearing loss, speech and language disorders, and more hours in the clinic learning to operate audiometers and read audiograms.
>
> And of course their requirement in statistics makes it possible for them to think that by talking knowingly about the means, medians, modes, standard deviations, and the rest of the differences between the test scores of hearing and deaf students they are saying something important.[26]

Hans G. Furth, a psychology professor at the Catholic University of America and the author of *Thinking without Language*, has observed that "the history of the deaf stands out as one exceptionally glaring instance of man's inability to see beyond the confines of his own theoretical assumptions."[27] From the

start, Bill Stokoe was an exception to the rule. He stepped outside the assumptions of his day to discover the differences between American Sign Language and the signed English that
teachers of the deaf were using — if they used any signs at all.

Stokoe realized that his deaf students must possess high intelligence to be accepted into Gallaudet despite having never been
taught in the sign with which they were most familiar and comfortable — their own language. He realized that deaf people were
perfectly capable of learning, that the problem they faced was not
lack of intelligence but a language barrier. Only when real communication between deaf and hearing people became possible
would deaf students arriving at Gallaudet, or any university, be
prepared to understand Chaucer or any other college text. As Bill
Stokoe wrote more than twenty-five years later, "The teacher
who learns signs and puts them into English phrases and sentences to teach Deaf pupils will fail to communicate, unless pupils
already have mastered the sentence-forming and the word-form-
ing systems of English — a most unlikely chance. Just seeing
signs that someone thinks stand for English words is by no means
the same as learning the word-systems of English."[28]

Bill Stokoe was coming to a realization that there was a relationship between his students' language and their performance.
He saw that their signs "were not simply slang; that when they
were combined in certain ways, they expressed meanings more
completely and in a more complex way than single signs or
words."

In the middle of his second year at Gallaudet, Stokoe talked
to Detmold about his observations:

> I remember telling George I thought there was much more
> to what the students and deaf members of the faculty were
> doing than just putting English words into signs or finger-
> spelling. I told him, it looks to me that they've got a real
> language here. Of course, I had been reading *Outline of
> English Structure* [by George L. Trager and Henry Lee
> Smith, Jr.], and I was thoroughly convinced of the rightness
> of their underlying premises that culture is a system, a seam-
> less web of a system, and that language is one of the sub-
> systems within it.

I just knew that when these deaf people were together and communicating with each other, what they were communicating with was a language, not somebody else's language; since it wasn't English, it must have been *their own* language. There was nothing "broken" or "inadequate" about it; they got on splendidly with it.[29]

Stokoe had read Trager and Smith's *Outline of English Structure* during his final year at Wells "while trying to cope with various neglected problems in Old English, Middle English, and Middle Scots." Soon after arriving at Gallaudet he began to notice, as he watched his students sign, that "signs with different meanings seemed to be alike in more ways than they differed."[30]

Many years later, in a conversation with linguist Charlotte Baker-Shenk, one of his closest colleagues at Gallaudet, he recalled that the students "weren't doing the signs the way I was taught to do them. Like the linguistic principle called *sandhi*, where the word in use changes because of the other words around it, the students' signs changed, too. Second, as I learned the signs, it struck me that they had the same kind of minimal pair opposition that you find in the words of a language you are studying — that they weren't simply iconic 'pictures in the air' as people said — but that they were organized symbols composed of discrete parts."[31]

George Detmold knew of Bill Stokoe's reputation at Cornell and Wells as a promising young scholar. As the newly appointed dean, Detmold was eager to see the Gallaudet faculty engage in research and scholarship. Furthermore, he wasn't particularly surprised by Stokoe's observations, which seemed to be a continuation of the language research that Stokoe had already done in graduate school and at Wells. But Stokoe's ideas stood in direct contrast to the beliefs about sign language that then prevailed at Gallaudet and other schools for the deaf. George Detmold recalls what Stokoe was up against:

Sign language at that time was something to be ashamed of. Even educated deaf people were ashamed of it — though among themselves, and in secret, they signed. Deaf children in school used it on the playground, and in the dormitory, but it was not permitted in their classrooms. In some schools they were punished if they were caught signing.

None of us at the time had any notion that sign language was anything but a visual coding of English. This is what we were told, by the experts, by people who had worked with the deaf all their lives. If deaf people, among themselves, used these signs in obviously different ways, which translated into some horribly garbled English order, that proved how lacking they were in "language."[32]

Detmold was supportive as always of his best friend, whom he considered "far and away the most brilliant and productive scholar ever claimed by Gallaudet." He encouraged Stokoe to pursue his observations, perhaps by finding a graduate student from the nearby Georgetown University School of Language and Linguistics who would be willing to use Gallaudet as a laboratory to study sign language.[33] Stokoe describes what happened when he went to Georgetown the very next day.

I was sent to the office of Professor William Austin. He welcomed me, listened intently for awhile, and became more and more excited as I tried to explain what sign language seemed to be. At the end he literally thrust me out of his office charged with orders, which for a mild-mannered man he almost shouted. I was to go around the corner at once to Earl Brockman's office and say that I must have a summer grant-in-aid from the American Council of Learned Societies; next I was to phone Trager and Smith in Buffalo and arrange to join their summer institute a few months later in 1957.[34]

In February of 1957 the Middle States Association granted Gallaudet accreditation and praised Detmold for the improvements: "Many personnel changes were made by adding new staff. The coming of the dean of the college aided greatly in its reorganization. Well educated, personable, deeply interested in the program of educating the deaf, he has been of special value in the recruitment of new staff members, and with the president has cooperated in the improvement of staff quality as well as quantity."

But the committee also noted that the new faculty, in order to be successful at a college such as Gallaudet, "must have some interest in and understanding of the problems of the hard of hearing. There is also the problem of communicating with signs, which does not seem to be as serious or as difficult to overcome as does the greater one of understanding the sociological and psychological problems of the hard of hearing."[35]

Stokoe's research plans made it possible for Detmold to report to the committee that one of his new faculty members was beginning a "structural linguistic analysis of the language of signs to see if sign language can be studied as other languages are with a descriptive grammar and lexicon."[36]

The summer Bill Stokoe spent in Buffalo working with Trager and Smith, two of the best known linguists in the country at that time, eventually led to his first written work, a monograph, about a topic that would consume him for the rest of his life: *Sign Language Structure: An Outline of the Visual Communication Systems of the American Deaf.*[37]

CHAPTER 4

· · · · · · ·

*Because it demands large-scale paradigm destruction . . . the
emergence of new theories is generally preceded by a period of
pronounced professional insecurity.*

THOMAS S. KUHN *The Structure of Scientific Revolutions*

Bill and Ruth Stokoe had grown to like Washington, D.C. Within months of their arrival they became members of the St. Andrew's Society of Washington, where Bill played the bagpipes. They joined the society's Scottish country dance group and attended the St. Andrew's Day ball each November. Some members of the society became their lifelong friends.

But the summers in Washington were another matter. The Stokoes found the heat and humidity disagreeable, especially since they both came from upstate New York where the days were cool and the evenings were, as Bill says, "downright cold sometimes — good sleeping weather."[1] The Stokoes welcomed the opportunity to leave Washington during the summer of 1957 so that Bill could attend the Buffalo linguistics seminar. They would enjoy staying with relatives, and Bill would be doing what he loved to do — studying and conversing with other intellectuals. Stokoe writes enthusiastically about that summer, which was, in many ways, one of the best times of his life.

Amazingly, for six weeks I would be in the company of the two men whose description of English had become a major focus of one part of my 1953–54 sabbatical study. It seemed too good to be true: I'd get a subsidy for what I was longing to do.

In his first lecture, Haxie Smith defined the subject matter by looking quickly over the subjects of physics, chemistry, biology, sociology, and psychology. The focus of our attention was to be culture, something none of the above investigated, and within culture, one of its ten major message systems called language. I had seldom been in the presence of a more inspiring teacher.

Besides the knowledge of how to analyze and describe an exotic language, I learned that in normal human interaction the information exchanged was preponderantly in the communication systems "surrounding" language. These systems, which Smith and Trager and Birdwhistle called *paralanguage* and *kinesics* (the one to be heard, the other seen), accounted for all but a fraction of what passed back and forth in face-to-face interaction. Our subject — language — was by comparison a minor channel for information. I learned also that language as a part of culture, though a very special part, is *learned behavior*, as is culture itself: to be human is to be a cultural animal, but to become enculturated in any particular culture demands direct experience and learning.

It was all this, of course, that formed my thinking as early as 1957. I had learned from Smith and Trager that the system used by members of a culture to carry on all the activities of that culture is a language. I had come into a community where deaf people communicated with one another in a rapid and apparently quite satisfying manner without any need to speak or hear: they had a culture of their own.

To be sure, in defining language as culturally based, Trager had said it was a system of vocal symbols. So it is for the great majority, but as early as that summer I began to develop the argument that (a) deaf people in each other's company most of the time share a culture; (b) such a culture differs from standard American culture (or any of its variants) because of a radical difference in physiological foundations; and (c) therefore, the system of gestural, not vocal, symbols used by deaf people is by definition a language. It was blindness to culture as a concept and inability to see cultural differences as anything but deficiencies that made those trained in speech and hearing, those most closely associated with deaf people, those who "educated" the deaf, unable to see what was so plain to one familiar with the anthropological thinking of Trager and Smith.

In that summer institute I also learned about systems thinking. The principle was simply that it is impossible to understand a system by isolating one of the components for detailed study while ignoring that component's contribution to the working of the system as well as the system's effect on it. The application of this to the study of sign language was first to be careful: the study needed many signers — not just one informant, but signers of different ages and different home backgrounds — and different kinds of interaction.

Above all, I could not act as expert or judge — I never learned the language to the degree that accomplished interpreters have. My task was to see how its users used the language, especially the contrasts and the equivalences they made. With these things and much more learned at the feet of genuine experts, I was equipped at least to start something new. All in all, it was a pivotal summer for my life and work.[2]

Without knowing it, Stokoe was about to start a revolution. Today his admirers, particularly linguists, equate his discoveries with those of Galileo and Einstein; they wonder why he hasn't received a Nobel prize. Many refer to Thomas Kuhn's theory of paradigm changes and scientific revolutions in connection with Stokoe's discoveries. But for a long time, most of the hearing faculty at Gallaudet didn't know what he was talking about, and most deaf users of American Sign Language were either incredulous or downright hostile. How could a hearing person whose area of expertise was Chaucer presume to do research on "the sign language" — signing was something that deaf people simply "did." As Padden and Humphries have noted, "It was simply unthinkable at the time to refer to signed language in the kind of terms used by modern linguists."[3]

But that's exactly what Bill Stokoe did. As soon as he returned to Gallaudet in the fall of 1957, he began to study his students' signs more closely. Gil Eastman, who was still a Gallaudet student at the time, remembers the confusion Stokoe's work engendered. As an example, he recounts the following exchange with a deaf professor early in 1958:

> Professor: Do you know that Dr. Stokoe is going to study sign language?
> [Eastman] Yes, he had better.
> Professor: I do not mean that he is learning sign language. He actually *studies* sign language.
> [Eastman] So?
> Professor: He is doing linguistic research.
> [Eastman] Linguistic?
> Professor: Study of language, science of language. He will analyze our sign language![4]

For the next three years, in addition to teaching classes at Gallaudet and chairing the English Department, Stokoe set about answering the question he had posed for himself: "What if sophisticated visual symbol systems were to be examined by the rigorous methodology of structural linguistics?" In April of 1960 he published his findings.

At first, Stokoe did not recognize the implications of his work. For him, it was an intellectual challenge, like the challenge of searching for the meaning of a single word in King Alfred's translation of Orosius. To solve that problem Stokoe had spent a summer examining charts, books, sailing directions, maps, and projections; it was hard work, but there was pleasure in it. Research was a habit, a way of living, ingrained from childhood. His father "had always insisted that [he] learn to do things thoroughly, the way they should be done, whether [the job] was farmwork or classwork."[5]

Instead of maps and projections, Stokoe began to study "the phonological, morphological, and semiological organization of signs." This time the intellectual challenge had human ramifications: his "brilliant deaf students were getting failing grades in English," and he still didn't know what to do about it.[6]

Stokoe remembers the three years between the summer in Buffalo and the publication of his *Sign Language Structure* (and his lesser-known textbook *The Calculus of Structure*, devised to help his students learn English through mathematical principles) as "a time when I was full of ideas, much more yeasty and less articulated probably than I can make them sound now." During those years, he was looking at the connections between linguistics and mathematics. "What brings the two 1960 books together," Stokoe says, "is the convergence in my mind of certain mathematical principles and the regularity found in languages. About the same time that I was seeing more and more regularity of a linguistic kind in my students' and deaf colleagues' signing, and getting George Detmold's approval to pursue research into the phenomenon, he was encouraging the math faculty to open the doors to the 'new math.'"[7]

Stokoe attended seminars and lectures on mathematical subjects. He read — and became enamored with — *The World of Mathematics: A Small Library of the Literature of Mathematics, from A'hmose the Scribe to Albert Einstein.*[8] In 1959, with Detmold's encouragement, he attended a conference in Los Angeles sponsored jointly by linguists and mathematicians. There he heard a presentation by Noam Chomsky, whose 1957 publication of *Syntactic Structures* had won him wide recognition in linguistic circles. Stokoe "had no idea who he was. That was soon remedied as I attended Linguistic Society meetings and read journals and realized that a revolution had taken place in linguistics. . . . I tried, of course, to read *Syntactic Structures*, but it seemed to fit neither what I'd learned from Smith and Trager about language nor my growing understanding of at least some mathematic principles."9

While Stokoe continued to explore linguistics, he was "still trying to help deaf students get the hang of English sentences." He and some colleagues attended meetings sponsored by the National Conference of Teachers of English. Again, Stokoe heard Chomsky speak, and he began to realize that Chomsky's fundamental theories were "making it possible for modern linguists to see both spoken and signed languages as coming from the brain."10

Stokoe became increasingly adept at recognizing aspects of American Sign Language that no one had paid much attention to before, and he began to realize just how detrimental that lack of attention had been for deaf students. He was losing patience with teachers who

spent their time complaining that the college shouldn't have let the students in because they didn't know how to write an English sentence and because their vocabulary was lacking and because their grammar was nowhere.

I remember once when one of the old-line teachers complained about her students at a faculty meeting with a psychiatrist who had become deaf and changed his practice to specialize in deaf patients. He was saying that deaf people are very self-reliant and independent, more so than his hearing patients. This teacher spoke up and said she found it to be just the opposite. She could tell her students to go for a job interview, and even if she wrote the information down, they might not turn up for the interview. Even in class, she said, when she'd ask a question, there wouldn't be anybody volunteering an answer, so she'd ask the question again.

As a member of the audience I stood up and said to the teacher, "How did you ask the question?" She said that, for instance, when she asked her students who was the author of *The Red and the Black*, she signed "who" with the finger at the mouth while she fingerspelled "was." I don't remember whether she fingerspelled "the" and "writer." She signed "write" and then made the body sign. "Red" and "black" were signed. Then with her finger she made a little question mark at the end. That was precisely the way I had been taught by Miss Benson to ask a question in signed English.

I looked at the teacher's signing and said, "You know, to a deaf student, you haven't asked a question at all. What you did is make a series of word signs and letter signs and then you dropped your hands as soon as you were finished. That is the way a declarative sentence ends in sign language. A person who relies on vision to know what's going on watches the face more than the hands. If you want to ask a question, when the signing is finished, keep the gaze straight, eye to eye, and the hands up, not right in front of the eyes but up high almost to neck level; that is the sign of a question. That pose is held for a split second. Any deaf person who knows sign language perceives that a question has been asked and that an answer is expected.

"On the other hand, when a teacher puts a question in English question-order and drops the hands and the gaze at the end of the performance, the student has been sent the signal 'I have just finished a sentence and am about to begin another.' No wonder you weren't getting any answers to your question — you hadn't asked a question."

That's the kind of thing our students had to put up with. I had just begun to discover the difference between a declarative sentence in sign language and an interrogative sentence. But these people had been there for years and years, and all they could or would do was make that little question mark sign at the end of their rambling, and they'd think that the students were too lazy or stupid or unmotivated to understand them. I had perceived that most of the syntactic signals of the students' sign language came from the face, head, and eye action, and not from the hands — but these teachers had perceived nothing but hearing loss and mental deficit and language deficit and all the rest of it.[11]

Stokoe's incredulity at the teacher's inability to communicate with her deaf students is understandable. But making a statement in public that had to be embarrassing to a teacher who had been at Gallaudet for many years could not have endeared him to that teacher, or to other faculty members, for that matter. Although it indicated passionate dedication, this kind of behavior, coupled with his friendship with George Detmold, alienated Stokoe's colleagues. Stokoe became convinced years later that he had been forced out of the chairmanship of the English Department because his colleagues misunderstood or disapproved of his research. But his unpopularity undoubtedly had something to do with his tendency to take a stand wherever and whenever he thought he was right, no matter what the consequences.

From 1957 to 1960, in addition to teaching, Stokoe again became the researcher. He studied the writings of the Abbé de l'Épée and other eighteenth-century French educators of the deaf. He admired their "open minds and boundless charity," but he came to believe that the basis of Épée's success was "an amazingly acute grasp of linguistic facts." Unlike other deaf educators of that period who taught "through articulatory exercises, ordinary writing, and a set of manual symbols corresponding to the letters of the alphabet," Épée relegated speech to a minor part of his program.[12] In *Sign Language Structure*, Stokoe expressed his admiration for Épée:

> The difference between Épée and all his predecessors as well as many who followed him is his open-minded recognition of the structure of the problem. He could see his own language objectively and analyze its grammar in a way which made possible its transmission to and synthesis in the mind of a bright teen-age, congenitally deaf pupil in two years. He could also see the mind of a pupil as a human mechanism functioning by means of a language, without being alarmed at the fact that until the education was complete that language was not French. His detractors seem to have treated pupils as automata into which the French language — that is, its pronunciation and orthography — could be built with the aid of suitable coding devices.
>
> Épée was the first to attempt to learn sign language, use it,

and make it the medium of instruction for teaching French language and culture to the deaf-mutes of his country.[13]

Stokoe observed that at Gallaudet it was as if Épée had never existed. No one, not even the deaf students and deaf faculty, believed that their signing was a suitable medium of instruction, much less a legitimate language. Many of the hearing faculty could barely use the language and were unaware that their students' grammatical errors resulted from the differences between their language and English. Stokoe put it mildly when he declared: "It is greatly to be regretted that from Épée's day to the present, his grasp of the structure of the situation of the congenitally deaf confronted with a language of hearing persons has escaped so many working in the same field."[14]

Lou Fant is less diplomatic in his assessment of the situation at Gallaudet at that time. Oralism had gained such a foothold, he says — at Gallaudet and elsewhere in the United States — that the deaf were lucky hearing people used signs at all. Sign certainly wasn't viewed as a language; it was "just the way you talk to deaf people." To challenge that premise was almost unthinkable:

> Gallaudet was the hub around which the education of deaf children spun. Its graduates went out into the countryside and became tomorrow's leaders. It had an august position and was extremely proud of that position. . . .
>
> It's hard now, in the wake of all that's happened, to understand the feeling that we had to work with oralism in order to improve the education of deaf children. It was as if we had to calm and allay the oralists' fears that "manual communication" deserved serious consideration, or else the world would come to an end in an Armageddon between the two philosophies. The war had been fought for so many years that, now that a kind of truce was in effect, we dared not jeopardize it. We handled the oralists with kid gloves, fearful that, like a bomb, they might explode and take us with them. That they did have power is true. They had friends in high places and lots of money to back them. We had only the truth, and we weren't too sure about that.[15]

Bill Stokoe was becoming more and more convinced of "the

truth," however. He had not risen through the ranks at Gallaudet; he was not a product of the "Normal" school network, which had produced the administrators and principals everyone was so chary of; he did not belong to the Rotary Club where most Gallaudet board members met for lunch; and he most certainly wasn't buying into the widely held oralist belief among educators of the deaf that to abandon speech was somehow to diminish the nobility of English. In support of his position, Stokoe reproduced, in *Sign Language Structure*, an entire paper by Anders Lunde entitled "The Sociology of the Deaf." Stokoe has described this paper, which Lunde delivered at a meeting in 1956, as "the pioneer work in the field." In the following passage Lunde remarks on the failure of oralist techniques:

> The deaf as a group fall into a completely unique category in society because of their unusual relation to the communication process and their subsequent adjustment to a social world in which most interpersonal communication is conducted through spoken language. No other group with a major physical handicap is so severely restricted in social intercourse. Other handicapped persons, even those with impaired vision, may normally learn to communicate through speech and engage in normal social relations. Congenitally deaf persons and those who have never learned speech through hearing (together representing the majority of the deaf population) never perceive or imitate sounds. Speech must be laboriously acquired and speechreading, insofar as individual skill permits, must be substituted for hearing if socially approved intercommunication is to take place. The rare mastery of these techniques never fully substitutes for language acquisition through hearing.[16]

Stokoe had begun to look at the formation of signs. As a counterpart to phonology, he created the term *chirology* — a word derived from the Greek word *chirologia*, the eighteenth- and nineteenth-century term for fingerspelling or signing. Stokoe also began to draw analogies between signed and spoken languages, observing that just as distinctive features in oral languages are "simultaneously combined to produce consonantal and vocalic segments," distinct signing parameters are produced simultaneously in various combinations to form signs.[17] Stokoe identified three types of parameters: designator or *dez* (handshape), tabulation or *tab* (location), and signation or *sig* (motion).

Stokoe's analysis provided a system for describing sign language. The system enabled him to show that the component parts of signs "have the same order of priority and importance as the segmental phonemes of speech."[18] It also provided — for the first time in history — a method by which sign language could be fully recorded.

Robbin Battison, the linguist who would later work with Stokoe at Gallaudet, explained Stokoe's careful process in arriving at this formulation:

> Bill was forced to take a good hard look at how signs are made: what parts of the body move or don't move, how the fingers bend or extend, how the hands contact the body, where they touch, the speed and repetition of movements. . . . In the end, he came up with a system that worked: he had nineteen different basic symbols for handshapes, twelve different basic symbols for locations, and twenty-four different basic symbols for types of movements. In much the same way that the symbols o 1 2 3 4 5 6 7 8 9 allow us to express any number, Stokoe now had a system that would allow him to express any sign on paper.[19]

Stokoe had developed a system whereby, for example, the differences between the words *mother*, *father*, and *fine* could be shown: although all three signs have the same handshape (dez), and the same movement (sig), their location (tab) on the signer's body is different. Just as sounds — vowels and consonants along with differences in intonation — are the elements of language received by the ear, so the shape of the hands, the placement of the hands, and the action of the hands are the elements that make the sign.

Stokoe observed that the elements are not combined arbitrarily. Rather, "in true linguistic fashion, the [sign] language allows for certain combinations of elements and not others. That is to say, the structure of morphemes in the system is not mathematical or mechanical but linguistic, and this level of organization truly constitutes the morphòcheremics of the language."[20]

In a study published in 1970, Stokoe drew further analogies between signed and spoken languages:

> Seen as a whole system . . . sign language is quite like English or any other language. Its elements contrast with each other, visibly instead of audibly. They combine in certain ways, not in others. These combinations, signs, "have meaning" as words or morphemes do. Constructions combining signs, like constructions combining words, express meanings more completely and complexly than single signs or words can. These constructions or syntactic structures are systematic, rule-governed structures.
>
> But there is a unique set of rules for making sign language constructions just as there is for making standard English constructions, non-standard English constructions, or the constructions of any language.[21]

With each analogy to English and other spoken languages, Stokoe further undermined long-held beliefs about "the sign language":

- that it was limited both in vocabulary and in its ability to produce grammatical sentences,
- that it was iconographic — nothing more than graphic pictures drawn in the air,
- that it resembled pantomime,
- that it was universal, and
- that it could not be used to express the abstract.

Stokoe was convinced that sign and speech were equal — and that both were manifestations of language.

By April of 1960, three years after his summer in Buffalo and only five years after he had joined the faculty of Gallaudet, Bill Stokoe had completed *Sign Language Structure*, which after giving a brief history of sign language "applied a rigorous linguistic methodology" to it. The paper also described Stokoe's method of transcription, to "expedite the study of any gestural communication with the depth and complexity characteristic of a language."[22]

In *Sign Language Structure* Stokoe took on Trager and Smith, his original mentors at the Buffalo seminar. While he continued to exhibit tremendous respect for their seniority and expertise, his own growing expertise in sign language studies led him to declare: "The sign language requires only a small, though radical, change in the definition of language given by Trager: it is the cultural system which employs certain of the visible actions of the face and hands, combines them into recurrent sequences, and arranges these sequences into systematic distribution in relation to each other and in reference to other cultural systems."[23]

In deference to Trager, who observed that Stokoe's "initial study did not yet prove that [American Sign Language] was a language," Stokoe conceded that "whether it is a language in the full meaning of the term is a question the linguist ought not to judge until much more evidence . . . is available." But as a teacher, as "one who works with the deaf," he knew that the question "was long ago settled pragmatically."[24]

It is difficult to measure and define the immediate impact of Stokoe's proclamation that the method deaf people were using to communicate among themselves was a genuine language. Even before the publication of his paper (and the subsequent publication of his *Dictionary of American Sign Language*), the oral-only method of instruction had begun to be recognized as a failure in this country, primarily by religious groups and by parents of deaf children who saw its dismal effects on their children's ability to learn.

By the 1940s, according to Mimi WheiPing Lou, many seminaries were teaching sign language to students who aspired to work with the deaf community.[25] And in the early 1960s Dorothy Shifflet, a high school teacher and hearing mother of a deaf daughter, developed a new system called "Total Approach." Hers was one of several sign systems that emerged at about the time that Stokoe was beginning to publicize his findings. All of these new systems, which continued to develop over the next twenty years, drew on Stokoe's research. (Ironically, many of the new systems undermined Stokoe's intention that American Sign Language be recognized as a true language to be used by and with deaf people. Although the systems employed ASL signs, the signs were used to perform a direct, word-for-word translation of English.)

However, as Stokoe's works became more widely disseminated, other professionals who recognized the superiority of sign language were able to cite them as the scientific "evidence" needed to support their experiences and observations — the "you could look it up" factor so important in convincing parents, teachers, administrators, and funding agencies of the need for change.

Furthermore, as Stokoe himself observed, Noam Chomsky had made the field of linguistics relatively popular; one result was a greater interest in Stokoe's research than perhaps would have existed before. As renowned linguists in the United States and Europe began to praise Stokoe's work, people who had refused to recognize the importance of signing, particularly educators and administrators, found it harder to ignore Stokoe's findings.

The early 1960s was a time of great change in the United States, as minority groups began to assert their rights to be recognized and respected. At the same time, the number of congenitally deaf students increased. The result was a large population of deaf people demanding their right to be recognized — not as handicapped but as a cultural minority.

While Stokoe's influence expanded in the outside world, at Gallaudet, he recalls, the effect of the publication of his paper was like that of Martin Luther's Ninety-five Theses posted on the door of the castle church in Wittenberg. Stokoe's publisher was the Department of Anthropology and Linguistics at the University of Buffalo — not exactly a hotbed of radicalism. But the reaction at Gallaudet was no less heated or hostile than that of Pope Leo X to Martin Luther. Stokoe was not excommunicated from Gallaudet, but had he been, many people wouldn't have minded. Gil Eastman recalls that "my colleagues and I laughed at Dr. Stokoe and his crazy project. It was impossible to analyze our sign language."[26] Robbin Battison explains why Stokoe's work inspired so much resistance:

> The first reason concerns the prevailing attitudes among educators of deaf people and deaf people themselves. At that

time, you must remember, sign language was only accepted if it could be justified as a contribution to the educational system. Any new idea about sign language was discussed as a tool for classroom use. As several stories have it, students and faculty at Gallaudet and at some residential schools mistakenly assumed that they were going to be forced to learn this new transcription system for signs, and that all their books would be written in these complex symbols. Of course, nothing could be further from the truth: the transcription system was intended as a scientific tool. But there were enough rumors and feelings going around to prevent anyone from really seeing the transcription system as Bill had intended it.[27]

In addition to *Sign Language Structure*, in 1960 Stokoe also published a 90-page textbook entitled *The Calculus of Structure*, which he described as "a manual for college students of English." It was a grammar book, intended to take advantage of the fact that many of Stokoe's deaf students were far more capable in math than in English.

It is difficult to evaluate the efficacy of this book (although Stokoe is still as proud of it as he is of *Sign Language Structure*). It was written in the late 1950s when instructors were teaching English to foreigners and foreign languages to English-speakers by comparing the grammar and syntax of the languages involved. Stokoe used a system of symbols throughout the book; simply understanding the symbols required enormous effort. A triangle connected to a diamond indicated a verb with no complement; a triangle with a line at the top, going to the right, next to but not attached to a diamond, indicated a verb and nominal complement; and a triangle with a line at the top, going to the left, next to but not attached to a diamond, indicated a verb and non-nominal complement. A square indicated "the end of nominal material used as subject, [followed by] verbal material"; a diamond indicated "the end of complementary material in predicate."

In the paragraph that followed his explanations of these shapes, Stokoe wrote: "It should be clear to the careful student of language structure that between the level of sentence parts, the level on which [these] symbols apply, and the level of words on which the symbols *n*, *v*, *ph*, *x*, etc., apply, there is another level of structure."[28]

Some of Stokoe's points were clear to no one but Stokoe himself. His good friend Carl Croneberg says he admired the book but used it in the classroom for only one semester, "out of a sense of duty to Bill. I used it one day a week in a three-day schedule, and I am pretty sure it was the day disliked most by both me and my students. *The Calculus* was a very logical and rational analysis of the elements of an English sentence, but at the end of the course I had absolutely no desire ever to use it again in a course. My students disliked *The Calculus* quite intensely and put up with it only for my sake, I believe. I cannot recall anyone, teachers in the department included, being enthusiastic about it."[29]

Bill Stokoe had both *Sign Language Structure* and *The Calculus of Structure* stocked in the Gallaudet bookstore. Many members of the faculty wondered just who Stokoe thought he was. He was supposed to be an English professor; how dare he presume to know enough about "the sign language" to analyze it? As Battison explains, "Although Bill was one of the few academically distinguished people at Gallaudet at that time, since he couldn't sign well, of course he wasn't highly regarded by the deaf people for the most part."[30]

As for *The Calculus of Structure*, a perfectly appropriate publication for an English professor, many English faculty accused him of pressuring them to use the book in their classes. Had Stokoe been at any other institution, the appearance of two of his books in the bookstore would have attracted little attention. But Gallaudet professors at that time did not regularly engage in research and publishing, and Bill Stokoe was George Detmold's best friend.

To make matters worse, in both publications Stokoe had given Detmold credit for helping him to secure research funding. Detmold's extraordinary efforts to win accreditation for the college had made him many enemies along the way. The faculty saw the publication of Stokoe's work as an occasion for venting their anger and frustration at the changes.

Jerome Schein, who was teaching at Gallaudet at the time, explains: "Bill's closeness to Detmold made many jealous.

[Moreover,] Bill was intellectually far above most of the members of the English Department. . . . As for Bill's research, it promoted ASL as a true language, something that, in the eyes of many in the department, demoted English. Since their livelihoods depended upon their English competencies, the English faculty felt threatened by Bill's research. Some deaf faculty felt the same."[31]

Lou Fant, who later came to appreciate the value of Stokoe's research, remembers the feelings of jealousy and resentment engendered by Stokoe's close relationship with Detmold:

I learned early on that [Bill] and George Detmold were very close friends. . . . I still have a memo I wrote to George proposing that the college establish a Department of Manual Communication. The department would, among other things, carry on research into "(a) improving the learning of manual communication and (b) exploring the effects of manual communication on the intellectual and social development of deaf children." (Notice the term "manual communication." That's how we referred to ASL in those days. It had a clinical, clean, academic sound to it.) Anyway, George sent me back a memo, and I quote it in its entirety: "Thank you very much for your memorandum concerning a Department of Manual Communication. I have not had time to study it as carefully as I should, but can assure you that I will give it the attention it deserves as soon as possible." My memo was four pages long and I felt slighted that he had given me such a curt, terse response. I concluded that he didn't think it deserved much of his attention. I never heard any more from George about my proposal — I like to think it was too far ahead of its time for serious consideration. What I thought at the time was that George sensed I was trying to move in on Bill's territory and he wasn't going to have any part of it. I chuckle now at the silliness of it all, but at the time I resented Bill because I blamed him and his pal, George, for nipping my idea in the bud without so much as a whole-page memo. The incident fueled my resentment of Bill and his work.[32]

Robert Panara recalls the reaction of the deaf faculty to Stokoe's work:

To tell the plain truth, most of us at Gallaudet at the time couldn't make heads or tails out of Stokoe's first book, *Sign Language Structure*. To most of us, it was a big joke and a waste of time and money. That was because none of us knew anything about the "linguistics of sign language"; it was a *lingua nova* to us. . . . We felt, why fool around with a language that you can't even handle? And why fix something that ain't broke?

Don't forget, too, that much of this attitude was related to a common dislike for the dean (Detmold), especially by the deaf staff, who had never forgiven him for what happened to Teddy Hughes. I would say this was the feeling for quite a few years.[33]

In addition to resenting Stokoe's friendship with Detmold, people on campus, deaf and hearing alike, were simply amazed by Stokoe's nerve. Lou Fant describes the faculty's response to *Sign Language Structure:*

Nobody, I mean not one soul . . . thought it was worth a tinker's dam, except, of course, George Detmold. The general attitude was this: Who did this whippersnapper, who had never met a deaf person before coming to Gallaudet, think he was? What could he tell those of us who had been around deaf people all our lives [Fant's parents are deaf] about "manual communication"? How dare he come out with such outlandish statements without first running them by the Old Guard to get their approval? Bill's sin was that he was an outsider, not one of the old boys' club — thus he couldn't possibly know very much. He was just out to make a name for himself with all this linguistic gibberish. ASL a language? Ridiculous.

It might help explain the negative reaction to Bill and his work if I can convey a sense of the period with regard to the education of deaf children. Oralism was the dominant philosophy of education. "Dominant" is perhaps too weak a word. It was the golden calf which, if we didn't all accept wholeheartedly and worship, at least we never publicly said might be a false idol. Those of us who were not oralists were timid about attacking it.

The quickest path to becoming a nonentity was to downgrade oralism. Young men, like myself, might just as well forget about becoming important in the field and wielding any influence at all unless we at least arrived at an accommodation with oralism. Even though we believed that "manual communication" ought to play a part in the education of deaf children, we nearly broke our backs bending over backwards to make it plain that we were in no way suggesting that oralism should be accorded a lesser status. We were the great compromisers, and he who could outcompromise the next fellow was the one who rose to the top of our profession.[34]

Stokoe's behavior was deemed so outlandish that the faculty demanded a meeting to hear an explanation. Just what was he doing, and who was paying for it? Today, more than thirty years later, it's hard to find anyone who remembers that meeting. It has become convenient, now that the logic and truth of Stokoe's discoveries are accepted, to say "I don't remember such a meeting," or "I remember that there was some sort of gathering, but I didn't attend," or "If there was a meeting, I don't think it was held to attack Bill."

Bill Stokoe remembers that meeting well. Initially he was flattered, believing that he was being asked to present his findings to the faculty — he even prepared a talk. But within minutes it became apparent that he and his ideas were under attack. George Detmold, who was also present and seated next to his best friend, describes the event:

> Bill stood up before them and tried valiantly to explain what he was doing, and what he had discovered, and valiantly replied to the angry questions that were hurled at him (you can really hurl a question in signs!). The deaf faculty were furious with him. He was a hearing person, a newcomer — how did he dare to publish anything about the deaf! It was absolutely ridiculous to analyze sign language; everyone knew that it could never be analyzed! Underneath all the imprecations you could detect a proprietary feeling among the deaf people that their most treasured and closely guarded secret was being brought out into the public view, to public shame.

The hearing faculty at this meeting never said Boo! and they never said Boo! later on, either. I don't know what they made of it. President Elstad, afterwards in his office, told me that I would have to stop Bill's work, and I explained that such a thing would be absolutely impossible even to consider.

It may be that I was pretty much the only one at Gallaudet who supported Bill. I don't know. The deaf people, ironically, were all bitterly opposed to his work, or to what they considered his work to be. The hearing people generally didn't understand (certainly not from that faculty meeting) what the fuss was all about, were too busy to inquire, didn't like a fuss anyhow, and were jealous of Bill because he was known as my best friend. They didn't mind seeing him have a bit of trouble.[35]

One incident that Detmold remembers from the meeting offers a crucial insight into Stokoe's personality and helps explain why, in the midst of such animosity, he continued his pioneering work: "Bill had learned what he was to call ASL . . . from continual observation. I remember an incident from that famous faculty meeting. Alan Crammatte [a Gallaudet professor] was on the stage delivering a blistering attack on Bill, and Bill whispered to me: 'Did you see what he did with his hand? Down like this? That means *not yet.*'"[36]

It was classic Bill Stokoe behavior. Ever the researcher, ever the student, ever the "stubborn Stokoe," in the midst of a concerted attack on his work he was fascinated by the way American Sign Language worked. His behavior was admirable, but it was infuriating, and it would earn him as many enemies along the way as his research did. In academia, as in the rest of this world, we like to see people squirm every once in a while. Not only didn't Stokoe squirm, he seemed utterly oblivious to the impact of his work on others. He maintained a dignity and a distance which were, under the circumstances, utterly incredible. As Lou Fant recalls,

As far as I could tell, it didn't faze him. He acted just like he always had. You'd never have known a storm of protest and resentment was swirling around him. You'd never have known anything was wrong by talking to or watching Bill. He just kept on pursuing his interest, thank God, and didn't let us get him down. Of course, I didn't know him intimately at the time, so I don't know what his true feelings were. On the outside he didn't seem any different, but on the inside? It must have hurt, but he never showed it, never even rebutted the criticism as far as I am aware.[37]

Stokoe did rebut the criticism, but in his own way, by proving in the end that he was right. As Robbin Battison explains: "He is one stubborn son of a bitch, and he sticks up for principles. I've never seen him back down from anything, I really never have. Gentle as he is, he sticks up for things he believes in and doesn't back down. It's kind of an interesting set of near contradictions, but that's Bill."[38]

CHAPTER 5

. . . .

The Dictionary of American Sign Language . . . *brought official and public recognition of a deeper aspect of Deaf people's lives: their culture.*

CAROL PADDEN

Although Bill Stokoe had no training as a linguist, within six months of the publication of *Sign Language Structure* he was invited to join the Washington Linguistics Club and to deliver an address there. "My pleasure in being here and my interest in getting to know all of you," he told the audience, "can perhaps best be measured by my temerity in accepting an invitation to meet you, to join you, and to speak to you, all on the same occasion."[1]

Hundreds of speeches, workshops, articles, and essays followed during the next thirty-five years as Stokoe's reputation spread throughout the United States and Europe. He soon stopped apologizing for his "temerity" — he had started a scientific revolution, and recognition of his achievement in the form of invitations poured in from the linguistic community. Gordon Hewes, an anthropologist noted for his research on the origins of human language, observed that "before Bill's work was published, few if any linguists or others considered ASL or any sign language as more than a crude derivative of spoken language, often ill-suited to intellectual communication. Most of the well-known linguists of the world regularly dismissed sign language systems as having little scientific significance. That they were useful for the profoundly deaf was acknowledged, but only as a substitute for 'real language,' (i.e., speech)."[2]

Stokoe had developed a new paradigm through which to view American Sign Language. While linguists embraced his findings and delighted in discussing their merits and applications, many people at Gallaudet and in the larger deaf-education community experienced the "period of pronounced professional insecurity" noted by Thomas Kuhn in *The Structure of Scientific Revolutions*.[3]

And that's putting it nicely. As prophesied by Dennis Cokely, a linguist who later worked with Stokoe at Gallaudet, Stokoe's work eventually undermined the "significant control" hearing people had gained over the lives of the deaf from the time oralism was introduced in this country.[4] As long as ASL was considered nothing more than a collection of primitive ideographic gestures, hearing people's superior role as the users and teachers of a "real" language was not questioned. These teachers, Stokoe observed, "had determined that there was nothing deaf people could teach them, and they had a lot to teach deaf people, so it was a one-way street."[5]

Stokoe recalls the reaction to *Sign Language Structure* among many educators: "If the reception of the first linguistic study of a sign language of the deaf community was chilly at Gallaudet, it was cryogenic in a large part of special education — at that time a closed corporation as hostile to sign language as it was ignorant of linguistics."[6]

Merv Garretson, a Gallaudet graduate who later served as a special assistant to the president of Gallaudet and became president of the National Association of the Deaf, recalls the immediate effect of Stokoe's work on him as a user of American Sign Language.

> Back in 1960 I was out West as a teacher and principal of the Montana School for the Deaf. Although we were somewhat isolated from the mainstream of happenings in deafness, we did get word that a gentleman by the name of William Stokoe had just published a "book on signs." . . .
>
> As a profoundly deaf individual who had received all of his education in a residential school, I was keenly aware of the importance of signs in our daily communication activities. Because of this, I had long been concerned about prevailing attitudes toward sign language. Through my [Gallaudet] college days, this concern grew into a deep resentment toward those educators who perceived sign language as "back-alley" talk, fit "only for bathrooms" and other private places, away from the scrutiny of the public eye. These attitudes were passed on to parents of young deaf children and to the media in various subtle and not-so-subtle ways. So when I learned about the work of Bill Stokoe, I felt an inner excitement. I ordered his book immediately. Somehow I had a feeling this man was going to light a fuse, bring to sign language a needed measure of recognition and dignity, and cause considerable controversy. . . . Here was someone, I dared to hope, who might blast open the pretense and ignorance of how deaf people communicate with each other; someone who would rock the boat and create waves in the field of deafness and in the Deaf community all over the world. I saw in Bill a potential

ally for all deaf persons who felt that signs were a necessary part of their lives, and who objected to other people's oppressive insensitivity to this fact.[7]

But Garretson wasn't speaking for all deaf people. Tom Humphries, a student at Gallaudet at the time Stokoe's paper was published, offers a possible explanation for the rejection of Stokoe's work by many deaf people:

> There were many who resented him for contributing to an ongoing and uncomfortable discussion about their language and proving to be right more often than wrong. Since many deaf people internalized the general negative view of ASL from hearing people, I think they felt as mystified and unbelieving as most hearing people did [in response to] Bill's work. Many deaf people attained status and what passed for power for a deaf person by continuing to put down "sign language" in favor of signing and speaking English well, and they were very threatened by any revelations that legitimized ASL. They tried to make Bill into some kind of crackpot to trivialize what he was doing.[8]

To understand why Stokoe continued his research despite criticism from most of his colleagues at Gallaudet, from other educators of the deaf, and even from deaf people themselves — criticism that persisted for almost twenty years — requires an understanding of his personality and temperament.

There is his intelligence, of course. Harlan Lane, author of *When the Mind Hears*, calls it "the high metabolic rate of his intellect."[9] Test results sent to Cornell from Stokoe's high school indicate an I.Q. of 150 to 155 — a range that indicates genius aptitude. But genius is not enough to explain why Stokoe sacrificed his cozy niche as a Chaucer scholar. It would have been far easier for him to teach three or four classes and go home at the end of the day to his wife and children.

Stokoe was always fascinated by new ideas, by new learning; friends and relatives remember that even at a very young age he liked to tinker with things to see how they worked. As a teenager he took his grandfather's rifles apart and rebuilt them to see if he could get them to shoot farther. He learned to fence in college; later he learned to fly; he became a licensed ham radio operator. He explains to anyone who will listen how bagpipes work. He writes poetry.

Humphries sees curiosity as a major motivator for Stokoe. "The thing that made it possible for Bill to do this work when few others would even think about it was the thing that sometimes led him a little astray. He really does like to explore ideas and theories that seem far out, and sometimes they turn out to be just that. Luckily for us, his theories about ASL were far out but not far off."[10]

Stokoe believes that his upbringing, perhaps more than anything else, is responsible for what he has accomplished. He was profoundly influenced by his parents, particularly his father, who instilled in him a respect for hard work and for learning. Although William C. Stokoe, Sr. (who was called Clarence), was a farmer, he had graduated from Cornell University; in his twenties and later, during World War II, he taught courses in agriculture. Bill Stokoe's parents taught him to read when he was three, "lying on my stomach on the living room floor with a book in front of me, spelling out a hard word to my mother or father, who pronounced it and told me what it meant." But Bill was also required to help with the chores: his father "had the greatest contempt for people who couldn't do a day's work in a day."[11]

Furthermore, Stokoe's father instilled in him a respect for others. Bill Stokoe has never forgotten the following incident:

> I was probably in my mid-thirties when I was driving one day with my father from Auburn to Aurora [New York]. Just beside the road there was a run-down farmhouse that looked as if it might never have been painted or repaired. The barn was even more dilapidated. There was a dog or two around, and there were farm implements rusting in the yard and on the porch. I had a Ph.D. from Cornell. I thought I was really something, so I pointed out to my father that here was a perfect example of life imitating art. It was a scene right out of *Li'l Abner*.
>
> Dad didn't react that way to it at all. What he saw was a

bent figure in bib overalls hobbling along the porch. All Dad said was, "The poor old guy." I felt very small after that. I had thought it was a funny example of rural poverty, but there wasn't anything funny about it, and my father knew that. That incident made me far more sensitive to human suffering, more sympathetic with the sufferer and less prone to find amusement in the externals. It certainly gives me pain whenever I think of it, that I may not be living up to my father's standard of judging people and circumstances.[12]

Stokoe's colleagues still remember with awe his ability to work for hours and hours without seeming tired. Edward Hall, who was an anthropology professor at Northwestern University while Stokoe taught at Gallaudet, describes Stokoe's work as "a gargantuan task. There aren't many Bill Stokoes in this world — people who are willing to spend the thousands of hours it takes to analyze a human communication system, and then record that analysis so that others can make use of it."[13]

But not even genius, curiosity, sensitivity, and energy fully explain why Stokoe persisted in defending and refining his theories. I. King Jordan expresses amazement at Stokoe's ability even to remain at Gallaudet under the circumstances, much less proceed with his research. Jordan's comments suggest a more fundamental reason for Stokoe's persistence. "He's really somebody who knows what he wants to do," Jordan says. "He's somebody who knows when he's on target, on track. No matter what the reaction is, he decides . . . what he's going to do and he does it. He just ignored the criticism and scorn and went ahead and did what he had to do."[14]

Jordan was referring to Stokoe's research on American Sign Language, but people who know Stokoe say he is that way about everything he does and always has been. His classmates in high school nicknamed him "Stubborn Stokoe" and "the Professor" because he would argue with the teachers if they thought he had given a wrong answer in class or on a test. If in fact his answer had been wrong, Stokoe would come back the next day explaining why he had been wrong and knowing more than the teacher about the correct answer. Stokoe says he still disagrees with Mr.

Richardson, the principal of his high school, about a 98% score Richardson gave him on the physics regents: "I still believe the answer he thought was wrong was the right answer," Stokoe says.[15]

Stokoe recalls that as a student at Cornell he once had a "discussion" with a man who was repairing his motorcycle. They disagreed about whether Stokoe's Harley Davidson was a 1920 or a 1922 model. When the man showed him the year stamped on the crank case, Stokoe had to admit he had been mistaken. But he says he justified his mistake by pointing out that "it did have 1922 wheels on it — after 1920, Harley wheels and tires were two inches wider."[16] Very few people care enough about such things to argue about them, much less remember the details more than fifty years later.

Stokoe behaved in much the same way at Gallaudet. Many people were put off by what one former administrator describes as his "petty persistence." But getting things straight matters to Stokoe, a self-described skeptic: "I have never been willing to take what somebody has said about something important without finding out for myself whether it was right or not."[17] Stokoe's colleague James Woodward describes this aspect of his personality as "intellectual intensity."[18] It may be this, most of all, that accounts for Stokoe's refusal to back down from his findings.

Robbin Battison sees a correlation between Stokoe's stubbornness and his pioneering role: "Bill was discovering new territory. . . . Maybe there was no one supporting him, but there was no one who could prove him wrong to his satisfaction, and that's all the reason he needed to proceed."[19]

Nowhere is Stokoe's refusal to let people stop him from doing what he wanted to do, what he believed in, clearer than in the way he fulfilled his passion for playing the bagpipes. Many people on campus teased him about the noise ("If the students weren't already deaf . . . "). Beyond the friendly jocularity, many people made cruel jokes about him, in his presence and behind his back, particularly when he dressed in his kilt, doublet, hose, and *skean dhu* and piped his heart out — uninvited — in some public place.

Bill Stokoe was not "a man on a white horse, but he didn't back down either," Jerome Schein says. Schein's most striking memory of Stokoe captures this aspect of his personality:

> I still carry the image of Bill practicing his bagpiping on the hilltop in back of the Hall Memorial Building. Distance from those who could hear was essential. Once a year, Bill would appear in kilts at Cannon's Steak House to pipe in the cele- bration of Robbie Burns's birthday or St. Patrick's Day. I recall his striding in, preceded by the skirling (skreechling?) of the bagpipes. He got a great deal of teasing and outright hostility for these musical onslaughts, but he bore it all with good humor — and did not curb his piping, which he clearly loved.
>
> Somehow I believe his [persistence in] his sign language research and his bagpiping betray a great inner-directedness, a core of equanimity that keeps Bill on track, pursuing the goals he knows are right, despite all sorts of adverse criticism and negative reactions. In this behavior, Bill is heroic.[20]

It would be many years before Stokoe was, as Carol Padden put it, "promoted to 'just possibly serious' from 'wacko.'"[21]

During those years Stokoe never stopped believing in what he was doing, and as always, he had the support of his best friend, George Detmold. Within months of the publication of *Sign Language Structure*, Stokoe, with Detmold's endorsement, was awarded a grant of $22,000 by the National Science Foun- dation, an enormous grant at that time. He would use the mon- ey, as reported in the college newspaper, "to continue his analy- sis of the sign language of the deaf in the United States. Professor Stokoe, Mr. Carl Croneberg, and Miss Dorothy Sue- oka [later Casterline] of the college will investigate the sentence patterns and the dialect differences of the language during the two-year period of the grant."[22] It was this research that ulti- mately led to the creation of the dictionary, which Robbin Bat- tison and others believe was "the most important thing that Stokoe created, the first true dictionary of sign language."[23]

Stokoe soon realized that to succeed in his work he would have to find deaf people willing and able to help him. His first choice was Carl Croneberg. Born in Sweden in 1930, Croneberg had lost his hearing at the age of twelve. In 1950 he heard about Gallaudet through the headmaster of his high school, who wrote a letter supporting his application for admission. In the spring of 1950, President Elstad, who was touring Europe, visited Croneberg in Sweden. Croneberg recalls that Elstad "examined my skills in speaking and reading English, and was satisfied. Next fall, I was at Gallaudet."[24]

By 1955 Croneberg had earned his B.A. in English from Gallaudet. In 1959 he completed an M.A. in English at Catholic University, becoming one of the first deaf people to receive a graduate degree from a "normal" school. However, the conditions were appalling: there were no interpreters ("no one had even thought of the idea yet," Croneberg says), and as he could not lipread he had to rely on fellow students to take notes for him. In some instances he didn't bother to attend class; he simply arranged to meet the student who was kind enough to take notes for him. "It wasn't exactly the ideal educational setting," he recalls, "but it was that or nothing for deaf students."[25]

While Croneberg was earning his M.A., Detmold hired him as an assistant in the English Department — part of Detmold's plan to hire qualified deaf faculty. In 1957 Croneberg was promoted to instructor, and in 1959 he became an assistant professor.

If Stokoe was impervious to the political and personal attacks on his research, Croneberg was practically oblivious: "I wasn't much interested in what others thought," he recalls. "We had a job to do and we did it. Period."[26]

Stokoe's other collaborator on the dictionary was a young student named Dorothy Sueoka Casterline, who had arrived at Gallaudet in 1955, the same year as Stokoe. Casterline recalls that Stokoe "taught Chaucer in my humanities course, and I was the only student in his nineteenth-century literature class — we'd meet in quiet corners in the Gallaudet Library." Like Croneberg, Casterline was not born deaf; she lost her hearing at the age of thirteen, when she was in the seventh grade.

I finished the seventh grade in public school, then entered Hawaii School for the Deaf and Blind and remained there for three or four years. I entered Gallaudet College (now University) ten years later. Hawaii School for the Deaf and Blind was an oral school, but students signed outside of classes. I was a day pupil and only picked up enough signs to get along with the other students. I learned to sign when I came to Gallaudet by picking it up; I never had any formal sign classes as they weren't offered to new students then.[27]

Stokoe's choice of colleagues was brilliant — and pragmatic. He knew from his linguistics studies in Buffalo that any study of sign language would need many informants of different ages and backgrounds. Croneberg had extraordinary facility with languages — he knew Swedish and German as well as English (ASL was his fourth language). Casterline had learned what ASL she knew outside the classroom — as did most deaf people — and she was familiar with various Hawaiian pidgins and creoles. Together, Croneberg and Casterline could provide access to other signers of the varied ages and backgrounds so important to a valid study. Equally important, at the time of the study Stokoe had been signing for only seven years — unless his collaborators were deaf people with whom he could communicate effectively, it would be impossible to proceed. Croneberg and Casterline were proficient enough in ASL to communicate with their deaf informants, and they were proficient enough in spoken and signed English to communicate their findings to Stokoe.

The dictionary took almost four years to complete. The grant money was limited, and Stokoe and Croneberg still had to teach their regular classes during the fall and spring semesters. As a result, most of the work on the dictionary was done during the summers.

Stokoe recalls that he decided to compile the dictionary partially in response to the criticism of his sign language research. The process also engaged his lifelong passion for tinkering with mechanical objects — including the motor of his childhood model trains and cameras borrowed from Eastman Kodak:

> If I was going to keep on with the exploration that so many at Gallaudet considered quixotic at best, at least I could compile a dictionary and standardize (so they thought) a language that exasperated and frustrated them by its chaotic variation.

At any rate, I accepted the inevitable, and the grants, and set to work compiling a dictionary, working, of course, with Carl and Dorothy. It was not, after all, so much a diversion as a long detour: anything we could learn about the grammar and syntax of the language could be built into the vocabulary entries.

I was familiar with the *Oxford English Dictionary* and renewed my acquaintance with Dr. Johnson's dictionary, from which I unashamedly borrowed the phrase "on linguistic principles." One concern was much on our minds. With colleagues insisting that a dictionary might "standardize" signing (to the great relief of myriads of classroom teachers), and with the question of dialects open, we tried to get material from as wide a base as possible. Sitting and signing conversationally for our borrowed (thanks to Eastman Kodak Company) camera (with a homemade motor drive — and a transformer from the electric train set I had saved from childhood), we managed to corner many different pairs of signers: students from elementary school and the preparatory classes, seniors and graduates, colleagues of several age brackets, native and foreign-born, male and female.

When the films were printed and run many times through our Moviola, Carl and Dorothy transcribed them in Stokoe notation and made an English translation. As in good lexicographic tradition, the "head words" were written on slips of paper in Dorothy's precise hand. She later operated the keyboard on the VariTyper machine, with a special type segment for the tab, dez, and sig symbols. We posted the slips on the blackboard on one wall of my office in the English Department, and the three of us met there to discuss them. We also had a room where the camera and subject chairs could remain set up for the odd moments of filming we could snatch from our own and our subjects' schedules.

Dorothy learned to use the slow-reacting VariTyper machine to set copy for the dictionary. I tinkered with the Kodak and Moviola, and Carl, at least for one summer and at other times, visited deaf centers within a hundred-mile radius of Washington, pursuing dialect differences. [The results of

Croneberg's investigations appear in two appendices to the dictionary.]

What makes the dictionary a viable reference is, I believe, our genuine attempt to "unlock" the language. By "linguistic" in the phrase "on linguistic principles" I meant describing the language people who used the language used. That is a deliberate tautology, which might better be expressed this way: describing the language used by members of Deaf culture, its signs, the way its signs are used in combination, the meanings they express, and the universe of knowledge the language represents.[28]

George Detmold remembers the excitement he felt when he first saw the dictionary:

I thought it a work of genius. It was a scholarly achievement not far from Samuel Johnson's. I knew of notational systems for recording physical movements in ballet but thought Bill's system more elegant and more significant. I thought it would have tremendous implications for deaf people, and for those who were associated with them, if now their sign language could be written. Most important, I thought, was that their language was treated here like any other language, with structural elements that could be described as they fitted together to convey meaning.[29]

Ursula Bellugi, a linguist and the director of the Laboratory for Language and Cognitive Studies at the Salk Institute in La Jolla, California, calls the dictionary "a landmark in the analysis of the special linguistic properties of signed languages." In a 1979 essay entitled "How Signs Express Complex Meanings," she explains the dictionary's value:

The *Dictionary of American Sign Language [DASL]* was significant in two ways: (1) it is the first extensive listing of signs of ASL with explanations of their meanings and usage, and (2) it is the first and most complete linguistic analysis of the sign into its component parts. It is not organized alphabetically but according to the elements of signs that Stokoe first identified and described. . . .

It is important to remember that the *DASL* is a pioneering

work, the work of one small lone group of investigators working over a period of a few years to collect the materials for a dictionary, for a language which had never before been written. These investigators were laying out the basic groundwork for a linguistic analysis at the same time as they were presenting the first detailed listing of the basic lexicon of a visual-gestural language.[30]

Although other books "listed the signs that deaf people use," Robbin Battison is convinced that "the *DASL* was remarkable for another reason: the signs were arranged according to a principle of the language. Just as spoken language dictionaries arrange their words alphabetically, Stokoe arranged his sign dictionary according to where [the signs] were made, what was active in them, and what it did. Thus, this idea that signs are complex objects with parts not only led to a writing system, but also led to a principle of *organizing* all the signs that could be related to each other, depending upon which parts they shared. This is like the way we think of different words as being related if they share the same sounds, particularly at the beginnings of words. This arrangement shows respect for the language."[31]

It was while compiling the dictionary that Stokoe, Croneberg, and Casterline began to refer to the language they were recording as "American sign language." Capitalization of the last two words, Stokoe explains, "came in with the times, as in the usage 'Black English.'" (Before that, he says, "we had been told that the formal name was 'the language of signs' — informally, it was just 'sign language.'")[32]

Many people outside the field of linguistics criticized the dictionary, however. Robbin Battison thinks the problem was "a strategic error on Bill's part. Bill gave new technical names to the things he was describing. Perhaps he didn't realize that he was creating resistance to learning when he gave complex names to simple and familiar things. He referred to *dez*, *tab*, and *sig* when he could have simply said *handshape*, *location*, and *movement*. Some people were probably put off by these strange words and had some difficulty learning what they meant and keeping them separate; I certainly did, and I worked hard at it."[33]

Dorothy Casterline, too, sees the complexity of the dictionary as the reason that the deaf community "didn't cotton to" it right away. "Linguistics is not an easy science," she explains, "and it wasn't and isn't easy to read the signs — it requires a lot of practice before you get the hang of it. We've always had (and still have) pictures to illustrate how a sign is made, so we've been conditioned to think of ASL as a picture language. Seeing these strange symbols for the first time can be daunting."[34]

In the introduction to the dictionary, Stokoe assures his readers that "the foregoing explanation of the system with the table of symbols should adequately introduce written signs to a user of American Sign Language." However, the twelve tab symbols, the nineteen dez symbols, and the twenty-four sig symbols, along with "a few additional symbols and some conventions," do not "make the notation more explicit" as Stokoe promised.[35] Rather, as one reviewer of the dictionary observes, "even a person fluent in the sign language would require considerable exposure to the notation system before he would be able to immediately recognize a transcription. And so the practical use of the dictionary will not be great at first, but for the time being it will be of theoretic use and interest."[36]

Despite the criticism, Stokoe's notational system made an enormous contribution to the recognition of American Sign Language as a genuine language of a cultural minority. But it took time. Lou Fant recalls that his own appreciation of Stokoe's insight dawned slowly:

> Four years after Bill's work was published, I decided to write a sign language textbook. I concluded that Bill had come up with at least one valuable thing about signs, and that was that each sign had three parts to it: the handshape, the place where the sign occurred, and the type of movement. I organized my book so that the signs in each lesson all had the same handshape, and only the place and movement varied. I felt this organization would facilitate learning the signs. . . .
>
> [Later] I left Gallaudet to become one of the founding members of the National Theatre of the Deaf [NTD]. Nearly all of the productions of the NTD were rendered in manually coded English, because ASL was considered bastardized English and not proper for use on the stage. Occasionally we

would throw in some colloquial expressions from "real sign language." That was our term for the signed language used by most adult deaf people when communicating among themselves. I did a monologue . . . in which I used "real sign language," and it caused some consternation among a couple of the members of the company. Somewhere in the recesses of my mind was a growing awareness that Bill was right, and that what we were calling "real sign language" was in fact ASL.[37]

After the publication of the dictionary Gil Eastman began to teach a course on American Sign Language and, at the same time, started translating English drama into ASL. In 1973 he wrote *Sign Me Alice* based on Shaw's *Pygmalion*. Referring to Stokoe's research, Eastman says, "Dr. Stokoe taught me to be aware of sign language and to appreciate its beauty. I developed sign language courses, wrote plays, and went all over the country to conduct workshops . . . and to give speeches about my work. But it was Bill Stokoe who helped me to develop pride in my language and my activities, and it was he who encouraged me to tell the truth."[38]

In 1977 a new course entitled "Structure of American Sign Language" was offered at Gallaudet for undergraduates and at the graduate level for faculty and staff. This was more than ten years after the publication of the dictionary. Although the impact of Bill's research was slow in coming, it was irreversible. "Prior to the publication of Bill's work," Fant recalls, "no one gave serious thought to a career as a sign language instructor. One could not even imagine conducting sober research on sign language."[39]

While in the beginning only a few people appreciated the dictionary's significance as the first linguistic analysis of sign language (one of Stokoe's most ardent supporters believed at the time that the dictionary was "the work of a madman"), even fewer recognized the importance of the essays in the appendix, particularly Croneberg's "Linguistic Community" and "Sign Language Dialects." The first is an ethnographic and sociological portrait of the deaf community for "the reader whose knowledge of the deaf is limited to having seen members of a group 'gesturing' to each other in an apparently very complicated way, or to having addressed a stranger but received only the response 'I am deaf.'" It is highly unlikely that such a reader would purchase *A Dictionary of American Sign Language Based on Linguistic Principles*. Perhaps that is why the essay received less attention than it deserved.

Nonetheless, it is an extraordinary essay. It presents a rich and realistic portrait of deaf people in America — something that in 1965 had never been done before (deaf people were generally portrayed in terms of deficiencies and differences). Not without irony, Croneberg describes deaf people as no different from other segments of the American population except in being unable to hear:

[The deaf person] is first and foremost an American in national and regional belonging, in education, in his way of earning a living, in his outlook on life, in his family and marriage patterns, in his recreational interests, in his successes and failures. He believes in democracy and detests communism and, like most Americans, is somewhat at a loss if asked to define the meaning of either of these terms. He knows he has to look out for himself if he is to survive in a fiercely competitive economic system. In religion he is a Protestant, Catholic, or Jew, or sometimes even an atheist. He marries a girl who is reasonably like himself in social class, education, and religion. Sometimes he has to resort to divorce, but there is nothing particularly un-American about this. He plays cards, invites his friends to a barbecue in his back yard in the suburbs, drives to the beach on Saturday, may read a paperback when he has nothing else to do, tinkers with tools and gadgets, talks to his men friends about women and cars, eats hot dogs, hamburgers, fried chicken, and ice cream. He owns a car and is sure he could not live without it. He may own a suburban house and then has the same problems with it as his hearing neighbor: a leaking roof, peeling paint, termites, mortgage payments, taxes. Like other Americans, he is determined that the lot of his children must be better than his. He is fully American. There are no other people on earth whose ways are so much like his own as are those of his hearing fellow Americans.

Croneberg proceeds to describe the ways in which deaf people *are* different, showing that the differences lie in behavioral patterns that constitute the cultural underpinnings of a minority group, primarily "the language of signs."[40]

Croneberg's second essay in the dictionary, "Sign Language Dialects," is the result of fieldwork he conducted in deaf communities in Virginia and Maryland:

> I had an asset as a sign language dialect researcher, a very special asset. I was deaf myself and thus a fellow "tribesman" to any informant I interviewed. I was also a Gallaudet graduate and a Gallaudet teacher, which meant that anywhere in the country I went to do the dialect work, I would be recognized not only as a fellow tribesman but as one enjoying special standing and respect in the tribe. In Virginia, due to my affiliation with my future wife, Eleanor, I had an even stronger affiliation with the tribe than elsewhere, which made it much easier for me to count on good relationships with both contacts and informants. A very large number of deaf people in the state knew and respected and liked Eleanor Wetzel; to be known as her husband-to-be was an obvious "in" no matter where I went in the state.[41]

With the publication of the dictionary in 1965, respect for Stokoe's work continued to grow in the linguistic community. In addition to invitations to deliver scores of lectures, he was invited to address the Seventeenth Annual Georgetown University Roundtable in Language and Linguistics in March of 1966 and the Columbia University Linguistics Circle in November of the same year. In 1967 he spoke at the Cued Speech Institute; in 1969 the Center for Applied Linguistics sponsored a two-day conference on sign language at which he was one of the featured speakers. In 1970 he published his first essay on sign language diglossia, which brought him even more recognition, and in 1971 he spoke at a seminar on deafness at New York University. With each presentation or article he further articulated, both for himself and others, his growing knowledge of American Sign Language. He had literally created a new field of research, and linguists from all over the United States and around the world were beginning to look to him for information and guidance.

Dorothy Casterline recalls being told by Barbara Kannapell (a Gallaudet student who later became a leading spokesperson for the rights of deaf people) that many in the deaf community viewed her, Croneberg, and Stokoe as pioneers. The dictionary, even more than *Sign Language Structure*, was the evidence needed "to show that deaf people can be studied as linguistic and cultural communities, and not only as unfortunate victims with similar physical and sensory pathologies."[42] The dictionary was cited in practically every article or book published about sign language from the moment it appeared — it even inspired the British Department of Education and Science to release a report entitled "The Education of Deaf Children: The Possible Place of Fingerspelling and Signing."

But it was business as usual at Gallaudet. Stokoe says that while *Sign Language Structure* had "gotten a lot of flak, the dictionary got nothing. With National Science Foundation funds we ordered 5,000 copies printed, more books than the Gallaudet bookstore at that time handled in several years. I suggested to the bookstore manager that we set a price and make room in the tiny bookstore for a display of the dictionary. But nothing came of that. The dictionaries were stashed away in cartons in a place where the leakage from an antique indoor swimming pool soaked a great many, ruining them."[43]

All the while, Stokoe continued to teach and to chair the English department. Soon after the dictionary was published he "completely revised" the syllabus for a graduate sign language syntax course he had decided to teach for the first time.

I had a class of six or seven students, one or two hearing and the rest deaf. I was trying to draw up a syllabus, but when I got down to it, I had to ask myself, what did I know about sign language syntax other than the fact that most of the syntactic signals were nonmanual? The students didn't have to hear me lecture about it; they could just read what I had written.

This was a two-year graduate program for people who wanted to teach the deaf. What did they really need to know, I kept asking myself. What would they have to do in the classroom to be effective? Certainly all the audiology stuff they were getting from the Department of Audiology was utterly useless. Why deaf people need audiology, anyway, is a little hard to determine if you ask me, because if they have been deaf since infancy or childhood and can get as far as Gallaudet, they really don't need to be given a complete description of the inner, middle, and outer ear; all the causes of deafness; the nature of congenital deafness; the kinds of syndromes that lead to it; which ones are carried dominantly and which recessively; which are sex-linked and things of that sort.

Then, of course, the Department of Audiology insisted that only hearing students were qualified for its Master of Science program, because graduates had to be able to hear the tones put out by the audiometer. Occasionally a deaf or severely hard-of-hearing student would challenge that point and say that they could always read the meters showing the level of the sound coming out. That was the kind of crap these future teachers were getting.

So I began to wonder if sign language syntax would be that much more useful if they weren't good teachers, if they didn't understand the way their students would learn, if they didn't understand the ways to make it possible and pleasant and relevant for their students to learn.[44]

At the time that Stokoe was planning the course, his son, Jim, sent him a copy of *How Children Learn* by John Holt. The book, a guide to creating a student-centered classroom, so impressed Stokoe that he "threw out the syllabus." He had his students read Holt's book instead, then observe deaf children being taught and write a term paper. One of the papers, written by Judy Williams, was published in *Sign Language Studies* and reprinted in *Sign and Culture*.

But Stokoe's class was an exception at Gallaudet. For the most part, he says, deaf graduate students were made to "jump through hoops."

The drawback of the two-year master's program in teaching was the way the students were tested. The written exam was not all that difficult for the students. The difficulty (for me at least) was sitting in on their oral examinations. The student faced three members of the graduate faculty, and I sometimes had to be one of them. I've never been so mentally put-upon, so emotionally disturbed. Sitting there and listening to the drivel coming from my colleagues in the education department, the inanity of the questions they asked, the complete revelation of their ignorance — not only ignorance but prejudice. It was almost more than I could bear. They would ask a deaf student questions about the function of the inner ear and things like that. I wanted to scream at them, "My God, the question you just asked is utterly absurd! You ought to turn in your resignation and go do something for which you're fitted."[45]

Stokoe never actually went that far in expressing his feelings, but he never went out of his way to keep them a secret, either. It was his nature to say what was on his mind, to act on his principles. These may be admirable qualities, but they were not qualities that made him easy to work with, particularly if one disagreed with him. His frankness, together with his high energy level, his intense interest in new theories and methods, and his passion for change and improvement, exasperated some members of the English Department.

Virginia Covington first worked in the department as Bill Stokoe's secretary; later, after completing her graduate work, she became a faculty member in the department. She was "able to understand his actions and behavior," she says, because she arrived at the office particularly early each morning, and

had the opportunity to see how Bill worked, something the rest of the department never had. I'd be there in the morning when he arrived and he'd say, "I read the most exciting book last night about transformational grammar, and I'm so excited about it," and he'd go on to describe it in great detail. And I'd say to myself, "Here we go again," because I knew the next step. And sure enough, when the other members of the department arrived, they wouldn't have had the advantage of hearing Bill describe his experiences as I had, and he'd just say, "I want everyone to read this transformational grammar book for teachers." They simply didn't know where he was coming from. He was so wildly enthusiastic about new ideas; he simply assumed we would be, too. He was always trying to see how things applied either to improving our teaching or to analyzing sign language. I don't think I've ever seen anyone who was more open to research. I mean he actually read this stuff while most of us were sitting around trying to figure out how to teach *a*, *an*, and *the*.

Bill was reading deeply in the field of linguistics, stuff that the rest of us either couldn't or didn't want to comprehend. Bill was so serious about all of this, one could almost say he was childlike in his enthusiasm. He simply couldn't comprehend that we were not as convinced as he. He really didn't understand it when people couldn't follow him. He was a true intellectual, fascinated by anything that had to do with language.

Covington remembers a particular project on which she, Stokoe, and several other members of the staff collaborated:

We could never connect. He was too theoretical, we were too practical. The generating English sentences project that we worked on was supposed to be a developmental text, but Bill was developing pages and pages of these complicated trees, diagrams that had been inspired by his reading of transformational grammar. We would spend hours watching him draw trees when we were trying to write grammar. Originally, Bill had been asked to get the book ready for the students to use as a grammar exercise book, but after a couple of years of doing the typing and editing, I just gave up. Bill rewrote the whole text. When the members of the department saw those trees and heard the term "transformational grammar," they branded it as "Bill's book," another *Calculus of Structure*, and wouldn't use it. Our feelings were really very hurt because the exercises were good. Some of the best teachers in the department had worked on that book, but by then we simply couldn't bring ourselves to do it over, to cut down the trees so to speak. So the thing just died.[46]

At about the same time, Stokoe invited the linguist Henry Lee Smith, Jr., one of his two original mentors in Buffalo, to visit Gallaudet and address the faculty of the English Department. "Bill was so excited about Smith's visit," one faculty member recalls, "but we simply didn't understand a word he was saying. And Bill was describing himself in articles and lectures as a linguist, something that we found a bit ostentatious."

By 1969 Bill Stokoe had been at Gallaudet for fourteen years. Perhaps he wished that his colleagues understood and supported his work, but he admitted only to feeling "a restlessness of a mild sort."[47] He applied for two positions: one as Dean of Arts and Sciences at State University College at Buffalo and one as Chairman of the English Department at State University College at Oswego. He was interviewed at Buffalo but was not offered the position. To most academics, Gallaudet was still a backwater for "handicapped" students, and although Stokoe's research had won recognition and respect among linguists, it is quite possible that those who interviewed him didn't know quite what to make of the man who had written the first dictionary of American Sign Language based on linguistic principles.

What is most amazing about Stokoe's job search is that George Detmold, his best friend and confidant, knew nothing about it. Stokoe's reticence on the subject exemplified what Detmold once described as "that other side of Bill, that very private side that kept him from telling me for almost five years that his only brother was dead."[48]

Stokoe's desire for change is understandable, particularly if one remembers that he and Ruth were from upstate New York. In 1962 Stokoe's mother had died, and now his father was seventy-nine years old and living alone on the family farm in Livingston County. It would be good to be closer to him. Ruth and Bill Stokoe's daughter, Helen, had gotten married in 1968 and was also living in upstate New York. In addition, many of Bill's and Ruth's aunts, uncles, and cousins still lived in western New York. Although Bill and Ruth Stokoe had established many close friendships in the Washington area, it would have been good to go home again.

CHAPTER 6

. . . .

You start to look around the country at work that's going on in American Sign Language now, and you realize a lot of those people either got their start or got a great deal of their training and experience in the Linguistics Research Laboratory.

I . KING JORDAN

As long as George Detmold was dean of Gallaudet, Bill Stokoe was shielded from the politics that affect most institutions. One example of this is Detmold's decision in 1960 to reject President Elstad's demand that Stokoe give up his sign language research: Detmold didn't even mention the incident to Stokoe. Detmold also protected his good friend from "the Great Powers in the education of the deaf" by serving as a kind of buffer. "In the 1960s," Detmold recalls, "President Elstad and I sat through a day-long meeting with them: S. Richard Silverman from the Central Institute for the Deaf at Washington University in St. Louis, Myklebust from Northwestern University, and Edna Levine from Teachers College of Columbia University and the Lexington School for the Deaf. The very idea that we should engage in deafness-related research was anathema to them. We were solemnly warned to leave all such research to those who were qualified to conduct it and not try to rise above our simple teaching mission."[1]

Detmold ignored such warnings and tried to make things as easy as possible for Bill Stokoe, in part because of their close friendship, of course, but primarily because he realized that Stokoe's "scholarly temperament and interests" could be satisfied at Gallaudet and would ultimately benefit the college:

> Of course, if Bill had published from the comfort of a research professorship at Harvard or Stanford, you may be sure that other university people would have paid quicker and closer attention to him.
>
> Yet I doubt that he could have done what he did anywhere but at Gallaudet. This was the only place that could give him access to a mature, educated, sophisticated deaf community, to the mature deaf language and culture. True, Gallaudet had no tradition of research, none of the laboratories, graduate assistants, grant writers, and the rest of the university research infrastructure. But I gave him all I could: space, time, assistants, and money, as he required, and it was enough.[2]

It was more than enough. Whenever Stokoe needed something, he bypassed the usual bureaucratic channels and simply asked the dean. The fact that the dictionary was the first book to be published by Gallaudet College Press is evidence of Stokoe's special status. Stokoe was well aware of the advantage in having the confidence and support of the dean. "For fifteen years under George Detmold," he says, "my wishes for staffing for the department or for research were always respected, whether the money came from the college budget or grants, and George turned overhead earned on the grants back to the proposal writer/principal investigator to use in pursuing the research."[3]

Under President Elstad, George Detmold had enormous control at Gallaudet College, and even those who disagreed with him conceded that he was an effective administrator. The charges of favoritism were somewhat tempered by the improvements Detmold made. In addition to guiding Gallaudet into the mainstream of accredited colleges, he instituted tenure and standing faculty committees and helped bring faculty and staff salaries and benefits in line with those of comparable institutions.

Even Robert Panara (the English professor Stokoe had replaced as chair) came to realize the value of Detmold's reforms. Panara recalls that when he applied to New York University's graduate school "the chairman . . . said he had never heard of Gallaudet, and that even though I had all A's in my so-called English major at Gallaudet, he could not possibly figure out how to give me equivalent credit since the school had no accreditation."[4]

In 1969 President Elstad retired and was replaced by Dr. Edward C. Merrill, Jr., who quickly decided that George Detmold "was too inflexible to assist me to meet some of the challenging goals that I had initiated."[5] George Detmold knew he "wouldn't last long" once President Merrill arrived. "About the first assignment he gave me was to check, personally, all the fire extinguishers on campus."[6]

It was a difficult time for Detmold. He was only fifty-two years old — too young to retire. He decided to resign as dean, take the year-long sabbatical to which he was entitled, and then return to Gallaudet as a professor of English and drama.

Bill Stokoe wasted no time in alienating the new president. He describes a meeting held within a month of Merrill's arrival:

The first time Merrill presided over a faculty meeting, he said one of the things he wanted to change was the "image" of the place. He said the thing he thought would be most effective would be to open the admissions to hearing students and then have an integrated campus. The faculty was incredulous.

I expect that one of the strongest speeches made against his proposal was delivered by yours truly. In fact, I made it so strong that as soon as the meeting was over and I got back to my office, I thought it over and I went down to the president's office and said: "I hope you understand there was nothing personal in this statement I made on the floor of the faculty meeting. It's just that my experiences have taught me that in educational settings, deaf people need a place where their mode of communication is respected and that this would go dead against the charter of the college which was set up to provide an education for people with so much hearing loss they couldn't get that education elsewhere." He said, "Bill, don't worry about it; I don't pay any attention to this. All faculty are alike. They don't like new ideas and don't want to go in a new direction, but if you prod them and drive them, they'll come along." At that point, I knew that he had nothing but contempt for the faculty.[7]

Bill Stokoe considered himself a man of principle, but many of the administrators at Gallaudet describe him instead as "not a team player." At times his behavior must have been infuriating to them. For example, soon after President Merrill arrived he sent a memo to the faculty asking them to lobby for the passage of a Senate bill to fund Gallaudet's Kendall School, a demonstration elementary school for deaf children. Instead, Stokoe wrote to his congressman: "My superior, whose salary comes in a U.S. Treasury check as mine does, has asked me to write urging passage of HR 18766. This I cannot do, for in my opinion the bill is ill-conceived." Stokoe argued that if the proposal were approved, the Kendall school, where enrollment was declining because of mainstreaming, would become "an almost empty multi-million-dollar showplace."[8] In the words of Michael Karchmer, Gallaudet's dean of graduate studies and research, "Bill Stokoe was an administrator's nightmare."[9]

It is no coincidence that Stokoe was voted out as chair of the English Department in 1971, the same year George Detmold took his sabbatical and was replaced by Acting Dean John Schuchman. For more than fifteen years, Stokoe's appointment had been renewed by Detmold, who as dean, was required to "consider" the recommendations of the department members in making the decision. At first, those recommendations were favorable to Stokoe. Dorothy Casterline describes the department during the early years of Stokoe's chairmanship as

> a nice place to work. I realize that I wasn't privy to all the interactions, political or otherwise, and I know we had some uncomfortable times. But by and large, we had a good group of people, and we were all friends. I still remember the whole department taking the English majors out to lunch. At that time we only had a few majors, and the department was small, so it was easily managed. In time, things changed; we had more students and more faculty members. I don't remember when we stopped the lunches, but I do remember that I was both on the receiving end as a student and on the giving end as an instructor, and how much fun it was.[10]

But Stokoe's popularity among the members of his department declined steadily for several years. Stokoe was aware of this, and explained it in this way:

> I insisted that exposure to good literature was really secondary to the task that faced us all with most of our students: to make sure that their ability to read English and their ability to write English had reached a point where they were competent to become critical consumers of literature. I kept insisting on that too much, and of course I was notorious for doing sign language research and belonging to the linguistics club. I suppose the other members of the department thought I was trying to make the Department of English into a Department of Linguistics. That wasn't the case, and I didn't insist that everybody use *The Calculus of Structure*, but I suppose there was some tension there.[11]

It was inevitable that the members of the department who had been there before Stokoe arrived would resent him, but by 1971 not many of those were left. Robert Panara had resigned in

1967 to become the first deaf faculty member of the National Technical Institute for the Deaf [NTID] at the Rochester Institute of Technology. (His career at NTID was stunning: he became the founder and first chairman of the English Department and the founder and first director of the Experimental Educational Theater Program there.) In fact, Stokoe had hired many of the members of the department who made the decision to replace him.

There are as many versions of what transpired as there are people involved. But it is clear enough that when Stokoe told Arden Neisser that his colleagues in the English department had "kicked me out" as a result of "the whole matter of ASL," there was only some truth to that statement.[12] Granted, Stokoe's determination to prove that ASL was a language could not have increased his popularity in the English Department. He was concentrating increasingly on linguistics and its application to teaching, and he expected his colleagues in the department to share his interest and enthusiasm; more and more, they resisted. James Woodward, then a teaching faculty member, recalls that "there was so much debate in the English Department about whether to offer a course in transformational and post-transformational approaches to grammar that it was tabled for over a year."[13]

Stokoe had always been perceived by many of his colleagues as eccentric, and some of them found his nonconformist behavior disconcerting: his piping, his fascination with sign language, his literary allusions, his seemingly inexhaustible range of interests — from making his own beer and bread to country dancing — and his habit of explaining them in great detail. To his supporters, Stokoe's somewhat impulsive behavior was part and parcel of his genius; to his detractors it was evidence of his lack of consideration for others.

Virginia Covington describes one instance of "typical Bill behavior." While still Stokoe's secretary she had her office across the hall from his.

I came in one day and he was moving me into his office — all my books, my desk, everything was moved into his office. I was just flabbergasted. He put up partitions and said, "Oh isn't this great?" He never asked me. I had no idea he was doing this.

He loved to redecorate. He used to tear down walls in the English department, change rooms around, install new partitions. There was a ladies' lounge next to what was then his office. I think he kept wanting to break through those walls and make that part of his office or make it the secretary's office. We really had to fight him on that.[14]

Then there was the matter of the department secretary. Members of the department recall her behavior as erratic, particularly the way she would scream obscene language at them if they didn't follow the office procedures she had instituted. But Stokoe thought she was misunderstood, that any "untoward" behavior on her part was simply the result of her dedication or of problems in her personal life. The other department members found his defense of her illogical, even absurd.

Most academic departments contain the stuff of which soap operas are made. This particular installment began with a complaint by the secretary that someone had been rifling through Stokoe's personal files — files that contained much of the sponsored research for the dictionary. Stokoe ordered the locks on the department door to be changed and issued a memo stating that "in order to protect college property, all key holders [were required to] sign a receipt and an acknowledgment of responsibility."[15] He committed a strategic error by having the locks changed over a weekend. Faculty with early Monday morning classes were infuriated when they found themselves locked out of the copy room. These actions destroyed any goodwill that still existed between Stokoe and the members of the department.

At about the same time, Stokoe discovered that personnel changes were being made without his knowledge. For example, one of the "key members" of the department had arranged with Dean Schuchman to transfer to another department without first consulting with Stokoe.

There followed two months of accusations, memos, telephone calls, secret meetings, votes of confidence or the lack thereof — a state of confusion comic in its predictability but sad in its consequences. With George Detmold gone, a group of faculty comprising more than half of the English Department met with Dean Schuchman in April 1971 to rescind their earlier recommendations of Stokoe as chairman and to nominate another candidate instead.

It was a painful time for Bill Stokoe. He had always perceived himself as a gentleman and a scholar, always prided himself on his ability to care for the members of his department. Like a father, he had encouraged them to go to graduate school, followed their progress, recommended them for tenure and raises. Virginia Covington recalls that Bill was "so thrilled" when she decided to enter a Ph.D. program that "he arranged for me to take a year off. He was really pleased and took it personally. Also, I think he was setting me up as an example to others."[16]

But in 1971, with many members of the department interpreting Stokoe's chivalry as paternalism, it was time for a change. The final decision was made at a meeting of the English Department held on April 15, 1971, a meeting Stokoe did not attend. With typical understatement, it was reported in the minutes, under item number six in a memo with nine items, that "the secretary was requested to send a letter to Dean Schuchman informing him of the department's new nomination for its chairman."[17]

This left Dean Schuchman in the uncomfortable position of having to inform Stokoe of the decision. At this point, Schuchman says, no one doubted that Stokoe "was a reputable scholar." It was "his administrative style, the fact that he could be arbitrary, that he wasn't a good chairman, that he had a temper and could be irrational," that the department members cited as the reason for wanting him replaced.[18] Stokoe recalls one final open faculty meeting in which he "stood up and tried to find out whether there were any with me. I defended my changing of the lock on the door on the grounds that some of this research involved human subjects and was sensitive material not to be open or accessed. Nothing came of that."[19]

John Schuchman remembers that, under the circumstances, Stokoe "handled it pretty well." But Bill Stokoe was no more willing to remain in the English Department under a new chairman than George Detmold had been willing to remain dean of the college — inspecting fire extinguishers.

Stokoe had tenure, and his research in American Sign Language was attracting worldwide attention and funding for Gallaudet; so a compromise was reached. Stokoe would continue to teach one course each semester (a requirement since his tenure was in the English department), but as Schuchman explains it, "a lab position was created for Bill as a way of finding a graceful solution to the problem. That's the way a lot of units were created at Gallaudet."[20] Bill Stokoe was being kicked upstairs.

It was a kick that was felt around the world, at least the world of sign language studies. The creation of the lab was arguably one of the most propitious events in history for the people who use and study American Sign Language.

Stokoe had never stopped trying to become a more effective teacher. However, his success was limited. He had been teaching the same courses for almost fifteen years, while increasingly devoting his time, energy, and talents to sign language research and the attendant study, analysis, writing, conference-going, speechmaking, and fundraising. At the time of his appointment as director of the Linguistics Research Laboratory (known from the moment of its inception as the "LRL" or simply "the lab"), Stokoe had just received grants from the National Institutes of Health and the National Science Foundation. He was now free to dedicate himself to the field of research that he had created, one that was growing rapidly as other linguists around the world began to use his findings as the basis of their own research.

Outside the classroom Stokoe made a far greater impact on deaf education than he could have as a teacher. An observation by Dennis Cokely in 1979 describes the pervasive influence of Stokoe's research: "[As] administrators and educators [of the deaf] . . . realize that policies . . . must be based upon the best available linguistic research in sign language and signed communication, this search leads directly to Stokoe's work over the past twenty years, since so many research efforts in this field are based, to a greater or lesser extent, on the efforts or ideas of Bill Stokoe."[21]

The Linguistics Research Laboratory (the name sounds impressive, but one must remember, after all, that Stokoe was still at Gallaudet) consisted of one room in one of the older buildings on campus. That didn't stop Stokoe; he was his usual indefatigable self. He and his secretary (he had been delighted when the lock-changing secretary from the English Department agreed to move to the lab with him) found some old desks and got to work.

Within months Stokoe had hired several researchers, to be paid with grant money. He again indulged his passion for redecorating — breaking down walls, building bookshelves and equipment stands — and complaining. "I kept telling Schuchman we needed more space because I had two grants coming in, lots of work to do, and research associates to hire from the grant and no place to put them. We were practically sitting in each other's laps."[22]

The lab was moved several times in order to give Stokoe and his growing research staff more space, but he had to fight for each move. He kept up a constant barrage of phone calls, memos, and visits to gain whatever facilities he could, leaving administrators frustrated and weary, particularly as many other departments on campus were also demanding more space. However, Stokoe's anger was often justifiable. During a particularly cold winter, radiator pipes burst, destroying books, equipment, and records. On another occasion, the maintenance department insisted that a leak in the roof had been repaired and would accept no responsibility for two floods that occurred in one week. In utter frustration, Stokoe "climbed out a window and took a photograph of the open hole in the slate roof."[23]

With the exception of Ursula Bellugi's Laboratory for Language and Cognitive Studies, which had been established the previous year at the Salk Institute in San Diego, Stokoe had no model for a laboratory where the primary focus was the study of sign language. And he had not been trained in linguistic research. That didn't stop him, however; he says he "just did what I had started out to do some time ago and enjoyed it so much it didn't seem like work."[24]

It was an extraordinary time, not just for Bill Stokoe and his researchers but for sign language studies. Any linguist in the country who was at all interested in the field knew of Stokoe's work and wanted to work with him. Robbin Battison recalls that although Stokoe offered him a generous salary to spend a summer at the lab, he would have traveled from California to Washington, D.C., to work with Stokoe without pay.

Initially, Stokoe wondered how he managed to attract these researchers to his lab. Soon, he realized what was happening: "I would send my proposals to the National Science Foundation and the National Institutes of Health, and the peers who reviewed the proposals would then tell other researchers and linguists in the field that I was being awarded a grant and perhaps they should contact me. That's how I managed to get Charlotte Baker-Shenk, Robbin Battison, James Woodward, Lynn Friedman, and others."[25]

Stokoe abandoned the traditional methods of research and turned directly to deaf informants to learn about deaf language and culture. Stokoe remembers that he and his researchers

were under pressure from the establishment from the very start. The president of the college and the superintendents of schools for the deaf had it in for us because we were a threat to them. We were always a kind of suspect operation. We were rebels; we were saying the emperor has no clothes on. We were saying that deaf people were real people: they can think, they can talk, they have brains. We in the LRL were perceived as "the lunatic fringe," and to a large degree we enjoyed being that.

I must say no one had the courage to confront me about our work. I got the feisty ones in the lab, the ones who were not content with the old-fashioned paradigms, with paying lip service to the philosophy of the 1880s. I got the people who saw what was going on, who wanted to go further into the examination of what was really happening, and who instinctively reacted against the kind of stuff they had been told about deaf people — that these people had a deficit, that there was something lacking, that they had to be cured, that deafness had to be prevented. That if you can't cure it or prevent it, then you've got to do the best you can, but you can't hope for much. We were against all of that — that's what directed our research.[26]

Stokoe still found time to chide the administration whenever he believed something needed change or correction. Merrill remembered that he "would occasionally receive a very caustic letter from Dr. Stokoe. If Dr. Stokoe disapproved of something, he would think about it for a week and then write me a classic, using all of his considerable literary skills."[27]

James Woodward, recalling his years with Stokoe in the LRL, remembers such behavior as counterproductive:

> Even if people did see the merit in Bill's work or in his criticisms, they had grown so accustomed to his heated memos about everything that they would simply say, "Oh, that's Bill," and not even consider his ideas. Bill was not very effective politically because he didn't realize that in politics, as in war, you always give people an out.
>
> Bill would say this [his behavior] was because of his Scottish ancestry, but I believe that it was because he believed so strongly in what he was doing that he perceived anything but a head-on confrontation as somehow devious. But is that the most effective way to get things changed — to attack people's point of view to such an extent that they feel the attack? Or is it to present alternatives?[28]

Gallaudet's current president, I. King Jordan, attributes the conflict between Stokoe and the administration to

> Bill's inability to play by the rules. He won't play politics and he won't play games. Sometimes in academe, as in other occupations and especially administrative organizations, the people who are in control play games. They say, here are the rules you're going to play by, and if you play by my rules and you respect what I'm doing, and if you're nice to me and tell me how wonderful I am, then you'll be rewarded. If you don't play by my rules, then you'll be punished.
>
> Bill didn't play games, and there were times when he was punished, when his situation in the university . . . wasn't enhanced and he didn't get the kind of support that he could have gotten if he had been willing to play along. Maybe he would have been able to do more work, maybe he would have

been able to achieve more, but I'm not sure he would have been able to sleep at night.[29]

Robbin Battison remembers an instance when Bill Stokoe "took on" one of the administrators. A number of new administrators had been appointed on campus, and Stokoe was making up titles for them, such as Dean of Parking Lots, Dean of Office Supplies, Dean of Enchiladas,

> — and it got a lot sillier than that. One of the deans brought a small delegation to the office to show them the lab, and there was a coffee cup sitting on the secretary's desk with the word "Bullshit" on it. This dean came back later and chewed Bill out for having a coffee cup that said "Bullshit" on it. Bill wasn't embarrassed at all. He just stood up to him and said, "Of course I have a right to have a coffee cup that says 'Bullshit' on it. Bullshit is the level of most of what goes on here at Gallaudet College."[30]

This "us versus them" mentality permeated the lab and may have contributed to its effectiveness, as like-minded young linguists gravitated toward the lab and joined Stokoe in questioning the established views of deafness. Some of the lab's researchers were deaf, themselves. No longer just the subjects of studies, they now initiated and directed studies and published the results — all with Bill Stokoe's encouragement. One of these researchers was Carol Padden, now a prominent interpreter of deaf culture. (Still in elementary school when *Sign Language Structure* came out, she is now a professor at the University of California, San Diego, and a member of the Gallaudet University Board of Trustees.) Padden recalls what it was like working in the lab with Stokoe in the late 1970s:

> I wrote to Bill while I was a freshman at California State University at Northridge explaining that I was transferring to Georgetown the following year and wanted some kind of part-time work in the lab. I was determined to pursue a career in linguistics, and I had heard that his lab was where things were happening. Bill got letters like this all the time, and I was just a nineteen-year-old with visions of a career in lin-

guistics. Bill — and this is something we all say about him — with typical generosity and graciousness, wrote back and said he just might have something for me. I should stop in and see him when I came back to Washington. I did, and he gave me a job for a project just funded by the National Science Foundation about social networks among deaf people.

You need to remember that my group came in at the very beginning of the legitimation of linguistics as a discipline applicable to deaf people — thanks to Bill Stokoe. Ursula Bellugi's group had published some new, inventive work, and the discipline was just starting to create its own space, and that made it easier on a lot of us young ones. We could ride on Bill's new transforming reputation, and it saved a lot of grief for us.

The administration, however, was generally hostile and just barely tolerant of Bill. How he managed to sustain a lab for as long as he did (and the fact that it closed so shortly after he retired is testimony to his tenacity and craftiness) still amazes me. We were always comparing the administration's attitude toward us with its support of the Cued Speech project (a truly wacko idea that continues to be wacko, and worse, truly harmful and disruptive). They got more extensive staff support than we did, got more equipment, got more space, more official recognition. We very quickly developed an us-them mentality. We revelled in our unusualness, held parties, and flaunted our status as the young turks from the lab. This did not go over well with our neighbors in College Hall. Continuing Education, one floor down, complained regularly that we were using space that could better be devoted to improving the reading skills of deaf adults.

I think most people at the time thought ASL was some kind of fiction. We (Bill and the other lab members) learned quickly how to behave like a minority. We spent much of our time in those early years giving workshops about the legitimacy of ASL, about the diglossic continuum, and how ASL had rules like all human languages. I gave workshops in the English Department and the Sign Communication Department on the new ideology of ASL as a name for the sign language that American Deaf people use (of course, at the time, I didn't *say* this — nor did I understand it in this way — just that I was teaching the "structure of ASL").

I think Bill's work, even before the lab, established ground rules for work on ASL. The work would need to draw from a certain tradition of commitment to data collection and analysis. It would need to divorce itself from the disciplines of education and policy and make ASL an object of study in and of itself. These new ground rules were extremely refreshing for someone like me who desperately wanted a life outside of deaf education. We felt shackled by the overbearing and oppressive presence of the "deaf educators," and Bill's work with all its unusualness (matching the way he dressed and how he furnished his office) just seemed like a way out. It was so new we thought we could make a new life for ourselves.

I think I was too young and too inexperienced to follow the details of management and power on campus. I do know that the president of the college at the time, Edward Merrill, barely tolerated the lab and regularly pitted Bill against Orin Cornett of the Cued Speech Lab for resources.

In Bill's lab we talked about self-determination, language, culture, identity, and throwing off the oppressive tradition of deaf education from the days when people couldn't bring themselves even to use the term "ASL." Bill created the possibility of liberation from old dogmas and, in his constant fighting with the administration, made clear the self-interest of the powers that be. Many of them are now gone, or have taken early retirement, hoping to supplement their incomes by consulting for their few old friends left in deaf education.[31]

Nowhere else in the world were deaf people recognized as linguists, as equals to hearing researchers. But hiring deaf researchers was just common sense to Bill Stokoe. He had expressed confidence in the capabilities of deaf people from the moment he arrived at Gallaudet, and he continued to do so as director of the lab. He told Gil Eastman that he could succeed in graduate school; he assured Dorothy Casterline that she was qualified to work with him on the dictionary; he gave Carol Padden a job in the lab before she had earned her undergraduate degree.

Charlotte Baker-Shenk, a linguist who worked with Stokoe in the LRL, believes this confidence in others, this utter lack of any feeling of superiority, was the most amazing thing about Stokoe. "Bill simply did not need control to be a leader," she says. "His philosophy was simple — I trust you, you are bright, creative, and self-initiating. He was there with his library, with his research, with his readiness to dialogue about any question. Bill was the epitome of true intellectual curiosity, ready to talk for hours and hours with anyone who wanted to talk to him."[32]

The "us versus them" mentality operated on more than one level, as the LRL was compared to other research labs. In 1970 Ursula Bellugi, who held a Ph.D. in education from Harvard University, became the director of the Laboratory for Language and Cognitive Studies at the Salk Institute for Biological Studies. While at Harvard, she had investigated the native acquisition of English by hearing children, and her interest had shifted to the acquisition of American Sign Language as a first language. She and her husband, Edward Klima, a professor of linguistics at the University of California, San Diego, had also been awarded several grants from the National Institutes of Health and the National Science Foundation. It was inevitable that Bellugi's and Stokoe's labs would be compared. "Competition" is too strong a word. According to Harlan Lane, the two labs differed in emphasis: Bellugi's focused on "ASL morphology and psycholinguistic issues"; Stokoe's pursued "anthropological linguistics" with an "emphasis on the phonology."[33]

There were differences in style as well. It was generally believed that Bellugi's people were more interested in collecting data than in promulgating changes that would benefit the deaf. By contrast, Stokoe's group took a strong interest in getting the word out about findings that could improve the status of deaf people. In 1972 when Mouton Press stopped publishing *Sign Language Studies*, a journal devoted exclusively to deaf issues, Stokoe decided to become the editor, and in 1975 he became the publisher as well. In 1972 he also began a newsletter, *Signs for Our Times*, which was circulated from the lab to more than a thousand readers. While Stokoe was quick, perhaps too quick, to publish new writings in the field (some said that quality suffered as a result), Bellugi's "camp" was faulted by some for being too slow to publish. Very little was published by the Laboratory for Language and Cognitive Studies until 1979, and in that year, when *The Signs of Language* came out, Ursula Bellugi admitted in the preface that "it is quite safe to say that we would still be revising the manuscript now had our editors not gently pried it loose from us."[34]

Differences in the day-to-day methods of operation in the two labs led Charlotte Baker-Shenk to distinguish between the "scarcity" and "plenty" models of research, applying the latter description to Stokoe's approach. But even Baker-Shenk found working with Stokoe somewhat frustrating at times:

> Remember, I was coming from that academic model that there is a limited amount of time, we've got to get going, we've got all these things that have to get done, we've got grant funding which we've got to account for, and sometimes we'd become very frustrated during conversations with Bill. I mean, could you please stay on the topic, could you please address these issues in a way that's not rambling and free association, but more of the scientific model that I wanted? I remember regularly feeling frustrated by that. Now that I'm a little bit older, I really appreciate that in a person.[35]

Baker-Shenk's comments mirror Stokoe's self-described philosophy in running the lab:

> I followed my own heart, and that's what I let the other people in the lab do. They came up with an idea and it looked like a good idea to me or looked like an idea that might turn out to be good if they put some work behind it. I don't know any other way of proceeding when you're doing real research.
>
> I mean, if the people in administration thought our job was to take an ancient paradigm and continue to supply data to support it, then that's not research as far as I'm concerned; that's just going through the motions.[36]

Putting "some work behind" what "looked like a good idea" wasn't standard research methodology. Robbin Battison remembers that "it took some getting used to," particularly when he and another researcher, Lynn Friedman, first arrived, having come straight from working on other sign language projects in California.

We had a large open office, as I recall, and we spent the whole first week sitting around talking very informally about whatever struck our fancy. At the end of the week Lynn and I looked at each other and said, he's not going to tell us to do anything — it's up to us.

We were right. Bill had a couple of research contracts that gave him the widest possible latitude to explore just about anything. I mean, it wasn't hypothesis-driven or anything like that. We essentially had to grope the whole summer towards result. We had to make it up on our own out of whole cloth. That was a new kind of challenge for us. We also learned something about Bill's character: he is not the sort of person to push something down your throat, intellectually or academically. I can't think of a single time when Bill Stokoe tried to persuade me to do something. Everything you did was perfectly okay. Everyone I had been used to at that point would have had a research program, would have had a conscious research strategy governed by a set of interlocking hypotheses that get proved or disproved, leading to new hypotheses as months and years go by and evidence accumulates. So this was a new style of operating for me.

It stemmed partly from the fact that Bill was a fellow of diverse talents. He probed many fields: literature, anthropology, sociology, linguistics. Linguists are very stuck-up people; we don't accept people who haven't gone through the same training we have and who haven't had the same theoretical grounding that we have. So while his work was inspiring, and while he laid down the groundwork for lots of linguistic work in ASL in the '60s, '70s, and '80s, and while he was cited by everyone because he had made certain milestone contributions, he wasn't the kind of person you'd go to for help in solving problems in linguistics. But he was the one who had defied most of the things written about deafness in the '60s by educators and psychologists, things that were absolute trash. This is one of the things we delighted in at the time, finding things that were written in textbooks about sign language which on the face of them were just totally absurd.

So he wasn't a linguist. But he was the one who created a place, the Linguistics Research Laboratory, where people could come and work, be guest researchers, and conduct linguistic or cultural investigations into the sign language of the deaf community. It was such a fertile time, such fertile ground for the transmission of knowledge and for the creation of knowledge. Bill managed to press on for intellectual honesty about these particular linguistic and cultural issues in the midst of a college community and linguistic and cultural community that should have realized all of this stuff but didn't.[37]

While he was director of the lab, Stokoe continued to teach at least one course per semester; he gave addresses at more than one hundred conferences; he edited and published a monthly newsletter, along with *Sign Language Studies*. James Woodward remembers that Stokoe was always at the lab during the week and often on weekends: "I wouldn't call him a workaholic, but he was working all the time. His work was a significant part of his life. We were a tightly knit group, particularly in the early years. We'd work all day, go out to supper together and talk, then come back and continue working."[38]

However, Stokoe was anything but a typical academic, burrowed in theories and research to the exclusion of everything around him. Dennis Cokely, a linguist who worked in the lab, found him "one of the most modest, friendly, helpful persons I've ever had the pleasure of knowing."[39] Virginia Covington recalls that Stokoe, while still chair of the English Department, would be working intensely, late in the evening in his office, when suddenly the phone would ring. "Here would be this mad tinkering genius, so to speak, working on what was to become the first dictionary of American Sign Language, and suddenly you'd hear him in this kind, contrite voice saying that oops, he had forgotten that it was marketing night, but he'd be right home."[40]

Ruth Stokoe had never learned how to drive, and Bill made himself available to her whenever she needed a ride. As the children grew older Ruth became more involved in her work as a volunteer docent at the National Gallery in Washington. Stokoe would regularly rush from campus to pick her up or drop her off.

Ruth did not become involved in her husband's work at Gallaudet; she never learned to sign, for example. But Stokoe preferred it that way. He liked having someone with whom he could share his other interests and relax, without reliving the politics and the problems. But when he did feel the need to complain, particularly during the period when he was voted out as chairman of the English Department, "she was a perfect listener to my woes . . . fully sympathetic and supportive."[41]

Stokoe's years at the lab, from 1970 until he retired in 1984, were exciting for both him and his wife. His fame was spreading, and he was invited to address linguistic audiences all over the world. He was in such demand as a speaker — and as a spokesman — for the recognition and use of American Sign Language, that he and Ruth often were unable to get home between speaking engagements. In a letter written in June of 1975 thanking one of his hosts for "a rich, satisfying symposium," Stokoe apologized for being unable to recall his reimbursable expenses in detail, saying, "I've just done the accounting for five trips with different details since May 10th."[42] During his time at the lab, in addition to being published in journals such as *Approaches to Semiotics* and *Current Anthropology*, Stokoe accepted invitations to lecture at more than thirty-five locations in the United States, Mexico, Israel, the Netherlands, Italy, Sweden, Denmark, and Germany.

When Stokoe was in town, the lab was not simply a place for research. Harlan Lane remembers "being welcomed there by him very warmly on several occasions. A lot of interesting people nested there and some colorful people were usually passing through on their way to or from an exotic place."[43]

The Linguistics Research Laboratory was nothing less than an international clearinghouse for the best and brightest in sign language research. Things happened in that lab that could not have happened anywhere else. Lane recalls the prestige Bill Stokoe brought to Gallaudet through his work: "During the years that I was a member of the National Science Foundation

Linguistics Panel, I believe that more research was funded on ASL than any other language save English. Gallaudet and Salk were clearly the foci of this nationwide movement of scholarship . . . which spread worldwide."[44]

Most of the people who have been influential in promoting the recognition and use of American Sign Language during the past forty years and who have published major works in the field either worked in the LRL or maintained close contact with it. Among these are Charlotte Baker-Shenk, whose descriptions of the nonmanual aspects of signing replaced the impressionistic notions that had previously been accepted, and Dennis Cokely, whose dissertation, "Toward A Sociolinguistic Model of the Interpreting Process," is still used in interpreter training and whose five-volume textbook, written with Baker-Shenk, offers a spiraling curriculum for teachers and students of American Sign Language. Today Baker-Shenk works as an advocate for deaf people in Washington, D.C., and Cokely is president of Sign Media, Inc., which produces videotapes for ASL instruction. Then there's Robbin Battison, whose dissertation, "Lexical Borrowing in American Sign Language," demonstrated that a language without sound can have a phonology. Others are Laura Pettito, whose research with deaf infants "babbling" in sign has received worldwide publicity; Carol Padden, who with her husband, Tom Humphries, has become a leading spokesperson for the rights of deaf people and the importance of recognizing them as a distinct cultural and linguistic group; James Woodward, whose anthropological work, especially writings such as *How You Gonna Get to Heaven if You Can't Talk with Jesus*, refute the pathological and medical models of deafness that have informed and directed so many traditional policies in deaf education; Harry Markowicz, who with Bernard Mottez coedited a French newsletter about sign language research and who studies the problems of deaf people as an ethnic group; Carol Erting, a Gallaudet scholar and researcher known for her work with the parents of deaf infants; and M. J. Bienvenu, who codirected the Bicultural Center, an organization (now closed) that advocated for the bilingual/bicultural approach in the education of deaf children.

These scholars and researchers did not simply work *for* Bill

Stokoe; they worked *with* him as part of a group of people who contributed to one another's knowledge and together changed the way that both deaf and hearing people perceived American Sign Language. Bill Stokoe was the catalyst for this group; his prestige brought in outside funding while the group laid the foundation for what eventually would be known as "the deaf culture movement."[45]

Nowhere was Stokoe's ability to recognize people's talents more evident than in the case of Judy Williams, a deaf graduate student and mother of two deaf children. As soon as Williams received her master's degree from Gallaudet in 1968, Stokoe convinced Dean Schuchman to let him hire her to teach prep classes in the English Department. At the same time, Williams enrolled her two children in the Kendall Nursery School on campus. Stokoe recalls that

> she turned the place around. The hearing mothers saw how Judy's children not only responded to her instructions but could communicate with each other and with the deaf people going along the corridors. The other mothers would ask, "What's going on here? These kids are oceans ahead of ours." Theirs, of course, were receiving auditory training — noises in their earphones, pictures, attempts to teach them reading and speech, making sounds, holding their fingers on the teacher's throat. And to give the teachers credit, they listened. Judy pointed out that she was using sign language at home to communicate with her children. That nursery school began using sign language practically overnight.
>
> Later, Judy Williams was one of the first to join me in the lab. . . . She made some incredible tapes of her daughter Tiffany at three and a half. Tiffany would address her father in American Sign Language, then Judy would ask her what she had said. Tiffany, who used signed English in the nursery school where her mother taught and read books in English with her mother at home, would code switch and address her mother in signs that were very close to English order. Judy wrote a wonderful essay about this, which I published in *Sign Language Studies* and later republished in *Sign and Culture*.

She was an utterly charming, delightful, brilliant person. A joy to work with, to be around, to look at, to see in action.[46]

Stokoe's friends remember that when Judy Williams was killed in 1975 by a drunk driver, he reacted as if he had lost a daughter. In a way he had. Stokoe was almost sixty — at least twice the age of anyone else in the lab. He did feel a fatherly pride in his researchers as he watched them build on his ideas to expand the body of knowledge of ASL — the subject that had consumed most of his energies for the past twenty years.

Stokoe's discoveries influenced linguists and anthropologists not directly involved in deaf education: Adam Kendon, who studied Australian aboriginal sign language; Beatrice and Allen Gardner, who did gesture-language-related research with chimpanzees; Gordon Hewes, who investigated the ultimate origins of human language; Edward Hall, who studied nonverbal communication. Stokoe met or communicated with these and other linguists regularly, earning even greater recognition as a result.

But Bill Stokoe's primary focus never shifted. He felt that his linguistic discoveries would be useless unless they were applied to the improvement of deaf education. In his speeches and writings, and in his pronouncements at Gallaudet, Stokoe insisted that deaf students were being shortchanged as long as educators and administrators continued to ignore the research he had initiated. In 1975, when Gallaudet began to direct funding into Cued Speech (a recently devised system by which deaf people were provided with manual cues to differentiate sounds that look the same on the lips), Stokoe wrote an essay in protest.

An observer outside the field of special education for the deaf might reasonably suppose that here at Gallaudet, if anywhere, sign language and research into its nature would flourish. However, the resolution adopted in Milan in 1880 by the International Congress of Educators of the Deaf has been questioned by some but never rejected by the established programs for the deaf in most countries. . . .

Research problems multiply when unsupported claims are preferred to scientific knowledge, but institutions *for* the deaf raise further problems, especially when they support research designed to show that sign language is a poor second-best to speaking, or that young deaf children may use signs at first but abandon them as they gain proficiency in "grammatical language." Like the general educational establishment, that for the deaf exists to fit every child to the — largely unexamined — norm. Hence it happens that much in print about sign languages comes from teachers of the deaf who give the impression that the signs they describe are only manually expressed code symbols for words (as fingerspelling is in fact a code for letters), and that "proper sign language" is the language of these teachers encoded manually. As long as languages differ and educators equate difference with deficit — of vocabulary, of language, of cognition — so long will genuine research into the nature of sign language encounter problems.

This attitude must change if sign language research is to continue and to have a proper effect. How deaf people communicate with each other is the crux of sign language research despite official neglect and opposition. Deafness, especially early in life, imposes a communicative situation which, since the species emerged, has resulted in evolution of several highly developed languages with visible instead of vocal transmission systems. A language and a special communicative situation imply a community. A community implies human beings: and if ever a group of human beings needed recognition by the educational establishment of its special situation, that group is the deaf.

Exactly that which official surveys, studies, and commission reports ignore, the sign language used by deaf people interacting, can be the key to improved life chances for these people. Research is now showing how and why the study, use, and official recognition of sign language can lead to better educational achievement, subcultural solidarity, and meaningful integration. It is time that educational establishments stopped their discouragement of research efforts and began to benefit by the knowledge it offers. Only by recognizing and respecting the integrity of linguistic and cultural minorities can a modern state win the loyalty and valuable contribution of such minorities to society as a whole.[47]

As Stokoe surrounded himself in the lab with the most knowledgeable linguists and researchers working in the field of ASL, he became firmly convinced that their findings should be applied in every classroom where deaf children gathered. Not to do so would be to short-circuit the children's futures. He reiterated his convictions at conferences, conventions, meetings, workshops: How could anyone confuse signed English with American Sign Language? One was a fully developed language, the other "not a language but a word-encoding system."[48]

Early in 1975, President Merrill, as national chairman of the Commission on Pedagogy of the Seventh Congress of the World Federation of the Deaf, sent a memo to all Gallaudet faculty asking for "input" on methods to better educate deaf children. Stokoe responded with an eloquent, incisive proposal outlining the ways in which deaf children could be educated, along with an accurate indictment of the practices then current in deaf education. This wasn't exactly what President Merrill had had in mind. Even today, almost twenty years later, "An Untried Experiment: Bicultural and Bilingual Education of Deaf Children" (reprinted below despite its length) is one of the most convincing arguments for the use of American Sign Language ever to be produced. Many people have observed that Stokoe's writings are often too scientific, too technical, to be comprehensible to the average reader. Even trained linguists complain about the codes Stokoe uses in his dictionary and textbook. But "An Untried Experiment" is Bill Stokoe at his best: pragmatic, convincing, and eloquent — advocating the cause to which he has dedicated his entire professional life.

In the long history of attempts by hearing persons and by official bodies to educate or to provide education for deaf persons, many methods have been tried. The history is well enough known not to need recounting here. However, one method has not yet been tried on any but an isolated individual or two, even though many findings of current science recommend it.

This untried experiment would begin with recognition that among deaf people in many places can be found a lively and viable subculture with a language sufficient to carry on all or almost all the activities necessary to any society. It would then utilize that language and the rich details of that culture as a means to bring deaf children into a full and satisfactory enculturation quite appropriate to their ages and their individual schedules of development. Next, as fully participating, though juvenile, members of the deaf community, they would be given by this experiment better knowledge of a central fact about the deaf subculture, namely, that there exists round about it a larger, dominant, majority, hearing, speaking, and (in some cases) literate general culture.

At this point comes the crucial part of the as-yet-untried experiment — the larger general culture and its language are made an object of study by the young deaf person. Unlike current educational efforts, this experiment would not immerse the deaf child from the start in a speaking, gesture-suppressing, near-blind milieu; that practice has all the humane virtues of hurling a naked Eskimo baby into the water between ice floes in the pious belief that sooner or later the Eskimo baby must learn to live in a watery world. Instead, in this experiment the society in which normality is not to hear would gradually show the youngster how the customs and actions and beliefs and words and rules of the hearing culture differ from the familiar ones of the deaf. Along with this process of getting to know about the world outside would go explanations of why knowledge of English in America, Italian in Italy, Danish in Denmark, etc., can benefit the deaf. In short, this untried experiment in pedagogy would be both bicultural and bilingual.

The chief reason for thinking it might actually succeed as few experiments in teaching the deaf have is that, since de l'Épée's time, many deaf persons have brilliantly succeeded in becoming bicultural and bilingual. Heretofore, these persons have had to achieve their double belonging and their skill at encoding language in two ways despite the educational system and despite almost complete separation between the two cultures. The number of truly bicultural deaf persons has never been large, because it is so easy for a deaf person educated in hearing society to share the hearer-speaker's contempt for "those deaf" who know only sign language and remain outside the general culture in obvious and in subtle ways.

As Vernon, Schreiber, Lieth, and others have told us, the deaf, around the world like other ethnic and linguistic minorities, now display deaf pride and are beginning to seize the reins of deaf power. Forty years have passed since Ruth Benedict's *Patterns of Culture* showed the world how much its human values and virtues depend on cultural wholes that define the integrity of a culture, and how empty are the values imposed by the rich and fortunate and powerful on those they colonize or otherwise enslave.

The term *slavery* is no hyperbole here. In primitive societies, slaves were kept to do tasks that slave owners thought beneath them. The Romans, more sophisticated, kept Greek slaves to teach them philosophy and art, but also to remind slaves and masters alike that Romans might be inferior to Greeks in the arts but Romans were the world's mightiest military, economic, and bureaucratic power. Today we have beaten the Romans at sophistication. Our counselors and rehabilitators and teachers and interpreters and psychologists and audiologists and so on do not keep slaves in the antique sense, but every one of them depends on more or fewer deaf clients or pupils or patients to make them feel important, successful, and superior. This is cultural colonialism, but the fact that it occurs inside our educational and other institutions and not at the ends of the earth makes it no less enslavement of members of one cultural group by the members and the ideologies of a dominant culture.

The time has come to try the experiment suggested here: Let the deaf community itself plan and operate the program of education for deaf children. Such a program would be at once tougher and more humane. Tougher because the most successful deaf persons, the deaf community's leaders, know better than anybody how important for the deaf access to the general culture and literacy in its language can be. But more humane, because an educational program centered in the deaf community would cure not only ills in special education but also the wasting disease of our whole educational effort; as Hall (1974) puts it, "A general failing of Northern European cultures, one that we are gradually overcoming, is our attempt to deal with virtually everything out of context."

Even reading, writing, and arithmetic, the "three Rs" of the past, which some educators want to go back to right now, are absurd in 1975 if they are taught in the fashion of 1880. For instance, in our recent affluence and technological explosion, the easy availability of pocket electronic calculators makes many school arithmetic drills and lessons a waste of time. But this technology could be used to make the abstract principles of number and counting and calculating much more interesting, because hours of paper and pencil work can be replaced by minutes of careful and intelligent key pressing. Again, the captioning of film and TV programs can make more material more completely available to deaf persons than ever can be done by efforts to improve hearing aids and individuals' lipreading skills. The fact is that culture is changing — not just the general culture of industrial nations. Yet enculturation for all who are not born into one of these cultures must proceed from full, comfortable, and satisfying participation in some viable subculture — we all have to start from where we are.

E. T. Hall (1974) has quantitative evidence of how much working-class blacks (WCB) and middle-class whites (MCW) differ on such basics as language, the use of the eyes, the sizing up of situations, attitudes toward questions, and expression of affect. In all this, one cultural difference is all-important: the MCW tries to read meaning in separable, out-of-context, discrete symbols, and tries to find the key to a situation in language: e.g., "But he said so and so." The WCB may find language a minor detail in the same situation: e.g., "Yeah, he said that, but he was lookin' way off and the other guy's brother was standin' right there, and did you see how he was shiftin' his feet and his shoulders?" The "meaning" that each of these observers finds in the same situation differs because of cultural difference.

In educational programs now in effect for deaf children,

the second kind of observation, i.e., reading the whole context for all its clues — the kind of observation deaf children are really good at — counts for nothing. The deaf child instead is forced to get just the sounds of language used, forgetting everything else. Then, if he finally gets the spoken and lipread sound right, he has made a dozen mistakes in grammar — meanwhile the whole rich context, the real meaning has disappeared.

If bicultural, bilingual education for the deaf by the deaf were ever to be tried, the inhumanity and inanity of present experiments in education would be first to go. Deaf children's skill at reading a whole context and their working knowledge of situations and people would be put to good use in learning. What they are good at — seeing actions in context — would help them do what must always be done if one cannot hear. They could then be led, as human beings secure in available society of others like themselves, to deal with the new contexts they must learn about. Using their skill at seeing, knowing, and understanding contexts involving people, they could begin to unravel the mystery of language as a system which relies much less on context for its information carrying. In a bicultural and bilingual setting, deaf children would set out to explore the working of spoken and written language from a secure and satisfying home base.

I believe this experiment deserves to be tried. The deaf community ought to set up schools in which the deaf greatly outnumber the hearing faculty and staff, if only as a balance to the circumstances that nine out of ten deaf children come from homes where only they cannot hear.

The deaf community should not just establish and control the schools deaf children go to; they should also control the preparation of deaf teachers. Deaf persons and hearing persons interested in the special education of the deaf should enter the classroom only when fully conversant with the deaf culture and language. Of course this means complete reversal of present practices, where in some schools the deaf teachers are allowed to teach the senior pupils, and all the preschool, kindergarten, and primary rooms are staffed by hearing, speaking, and mouthing teachers who know nothing of the world of deafness. In this untried experiment it would be only the exceptional hearing person who could work with the youngest children; while most hearing-speaking teachers would be most usefully employed in the later grades helping the pupils learn more about the hearing-speaking world they will soon see more of. But the babies would start off with adults who, like themselves, have to cope with the world through information entering the eyes, transmitted by bodily action, but generated and organized by good deaf brains.

As for the parents, let the hearing parents learn how to fingerspell and sign, if they like. Many are doing so now as part of the program of "total communication." But let the school make it possible for the children to interact freely in "deaf" Sign. There will be plenty of time later for them to pick up the different ways of manually representing the majority culture's language. In fact they pick up now various approximations, in large part, I believe, because the schools still do not recognize that there are varieties of majority language, varieties of sign language, and varieties of ways of mixing the two.

There will be time for real learning and developing and second-culture-language learning in a school where it is natural as breathing not to hear. In a world where there is much to see and where it is natural to sign and beautiful to be deaf and alive, there will be time to learn that language is made inside the head whether it comes out as English or Sign.

There may be plenty of time for the deaf child, but I would like to see this experiment tried soon. Not just because a cultural minority with a silent language needs a chance to catch up with the majority's world, but also because if the majority could let this experiment be tried soon enough it might just break the self-destructive, dehumanizing spiral it seems locked into.[49]

Needless to say, President Merrill did not advocate the adoption of Bill Stokoe's "untried experiment" at the Seventh Congress of the World Federation of the Deaf. In fact, he never responded to it at all.

CHAPTER 7

. . . .

*The first time I was aware of the Gallaudet response to Bill was when
the school was considering closing his lab. I was dumbfounded —
imagine closing Jonas Salk's lab after he had discovered his vaccine! I
wrote the most persuasive letter of which I was capable, but arguments
were beside the point; politics were to the point.*

HARLAN LANE

Although Bill Stokoe was able to put the English Department episode behind him, and although he was "satisfied and stimulated" in his role as director of the Gallaudet Linguistics Research Lab, the early 1970s were very difficult years for him. In 1970 Helen Stokoe Phillips gave birth to a daughter, Jennifer, and although Bill and Ruth Stokoe were thrilled to be grandparents, they knew that their daughter was struggling to make her marriage work. In 1971 Bill's eighty-three-year-old father, Clarence, lost sight in one eye during cataract surgery. When Stokoe visited him in the hospital, he "could see that the shock of surgery and its sequel had left him weakened."[1]

By the end of 1972, Stokoe's aging aunts were no longer able to care for his father, so Bill and Ruth brought him to their home and gave him their daughter's old room. It was a difficult time for everyone. "Dad hated to be dependent; Ruth and I often disagreed about what was to be done, both in the long term and over little, immediate problems."[2] Bill soon found a suitable senior citizen residence less than two miles away where his father could have a private kitchenette, with the option of using the common dining room. His father quickly made friends there, and Stokoe stopped in every day on his way to or from Gallaudet. For a short while, Bill Stokoe believed that "Dad was himself again, in charge."[3]

Stokoe was so confident of his father's recovery that he and Ruth took a previously scheduled trip to Israel, where Bill had been invited to present a paper. However, almost immediately after they returned, Clarence Stokoe suffered another stroke and died on April 28, 1973. It was a terrific blow for Stokoe. He had idolized his father, and he began to wonder whether he had done enough to help him during his mother's final long illness; he wondered how his parents had been able to bear the death of their twenty-two-year-old son Jim in 1942. He recalled his father's devotion: "Nothing made him happier than good things happening to me and the children."[4]

More than ever, Stokoe devoted himself to the lab; he spent endless hours there. The esprit de corps of the lab helped him to deal with his father's death, an event that he described as "the greatest loss I ever endured."[5] The people in the lab were friends as well as colleagues. Stokoe viewed their successes in much the same way that his father had viewed his children's successes. Baker-Shenk recalls that Stokoe gave her "all the support and affirmation I needed to build my confidence. He was in many ways like a father. . . . We could make mistakes with each other, but you always felt that Bill's love for you was unconditional. You don't often find such conditions where you work."[6] Dennis Cokely recalls that Stokoe often brought his home-baked bread and home-brewed beer into the lab "for sampling."[7] Harry Markowicz, who joined the lab in 1973, remembers picnics, gatherings, and celebrations of many occasions. Stokoe often invited his colleagues to his home for dinner, and they frequently went out to lunch together. Bill and Ruth Stokoe, along with other members of the lab, attended Charlotte Baker-Shenk's wedding. In 1974 a party was held to bid farewell to the lock-changing secretary who had come with Stokoe from the English Department. "We were all rather relieved to see her go," Markowicz says, "but there was Bill, sentimental as ever, with tears in his eyes."[8]

According to Robbin Battison, it was in the lab that Stokoe acquired his "name sign." It is common for deaf people to create name signs to avoid the time-consuming process of fingerspelling. Often, the name sign reflects a significant characteristic of the person. Bill Stokoe's hair is extremely thick; in those days, when he didn't have it all cut off in a crew cut, he often wore it in "a kind of bowl haircut, almost medieval," Battison recalls. "We had a deaf student working with us in the lab, Hedy Udkovich. One day she referred to Bill by placing her open hand, with all the fingers extended, palm down, on the top of her head so that the fingers drooped over her forehead. That particular name sign stuck, and it's the one Bill still has today."[9]

Stokoe's youthful appearance has always been a source of amazement to people. Even today he is slim, straight, and strong, with a handsome face many describe as boyish. In 1975, at the age of fifty-six, he prided himself on his ability to beat Baker-Shenk at tennis, particularly since she was "so slim, strong, and athletic, a real California type."[10]

Stokoe's youthfulness is not limited to his physical appearance. Virginia Volterra, an Italian linguist who has worked and corresponded with Stokoe over the years, recalls that he "was very attentive to new ideas, to new possibilities, to new suggestions. He was curious about any novelty; he was never attached to old ideas. Even with his own work he was ready to criticize, to find that it didn't work anymore. It is really extremely rare to find something like that, even in a young person. It's an incredible advantage that Bill has, an advantage that has benefitted his research and the field in general."[11]

Stokoe has never lost his youthful idealism. Leon Auerbach, a deaf Gallaudet professor, recalls an incident in which

> Bill was, as always, a great friend of deaf people. I got an invitation to speak on the topic of teaching mathematics to Deaf children at a convention sponsored by an oral group called, I think, the Bell Speech Association of New York City. I replied saying that I would be happy to read a paper at the convention provided I could do it in sign language since my speech is virtually nonexistent. Soon afterwards, I received a letter withdrawing the invitation! Meanwhile, I had mentioned the matter to Bill Stokoe.
>
> Shortly thereafter, the same group invited him to read a paper on the same topic. "Given the circumstances of your treatment of Professor Leon Auerbach," he replied, "I decline the invitation." I really appreciated his support.[12]

But Stokoe had his detractors as well. One former colleague found it amusing that Stokoe had stopped calling himself an English professor and became a self-described "linguist." Former Gallaudet president Edward Merrill, a fellow member of the prestigious Cosmos Club in Washington, D.C., noted that Stokoe listed himself in the club's directory as an anthropologist. Merrill was convinced that Stokoe made life much harder than necessary for himself and for those around him: "He was narrow in his understanding and grasp of the complexities of an entire system in its political setting. He was not an easy person to work with."[13]

This criticism cannot be discounted entirely. Even Stokoe's good friends and supporters saw his confrontational style as sometimes counterproductive in relation to his work. To all appearances, Stokoe simply did not care whether people liked or approved of him; he tended to perceive criticism of him or his work as evidence of a defect in the critic. At the same time, however, he was fiercely loyal to his friends, never abandoning them; his support of his secretary from the English Department is only one example. Once Stokoe had taken someone under his wing — or once someone exhibited loyalty to him — there was no doubt that he would support that person, even if it took personal or professional sacrifice.

Stokoe's reactions to people he considered unfair or illogical were equally strong: he criticized them without reserve, with little concern for the effect his criticism had on them and even less concern for the consequences to himself or his interests. There was no middle ground with Bill Stokoe; people either adored or despised him.

Although Stokoe antagonized many of the administrators at Gallaudet, he continued to attract funding and topflight linguists to the lab. These linguists were taking his ideas and branching out with them, and in some ways they were leaving Stokoe behind. Carol Padden explains that this was almost inevitable:

> With respect to sign language linguistics, I think at some point the discipline took off in directions that Bill couldn't, or rather, didn't want to, pursue. His seminal work on phonological structure spawned a very complex field of sign language phonology that, ironically, I don't think Bill fully understands (for example, the work of Perlmutter, Liddell and Johnson, Sandler, Brentari, Corina). He gave a keynote talk at the Gallaudet International Sign Language Research Conference during which he wondered whether this new complexity and abstraction were worth the trouble. He called for a return to meaningful research, and the feeling I had was that he wasn't a part of the very modern discipline of sign language linguistics. But it should be said that sign phonology today has reached a level of such complexity and detail that it has left a lot of compatriots scratching their heads, not just Bill.[14]

Robbin Battison thinks that Stokoe's lack of formal training in linguistics probably contributed to his ability to see what no one else had seen before, but that eventually it held him back as his linguistic audience became more sophisticated.

In the late '60s and early '70s Stokoe was the only person who had published any work whatsoever in sign language linguistics that had stood the test of time. Bill should be seen as the trailblazer; he identified and constrained the problem for other linguistic researchers. But over time, I began to realize that Bill was interested in exploring only certain research questions and that he was a bit flighty in his research. You know, he went from being an English professor to a linguist to an anthropologist in one decade. I think in some cases he would choose what interested him, and that was a limitation. He certainly didn't lack for zeal, but Bill could only see part of the picture at one time.[15]

There may be some truth in these observations. Stokoe's articles and speeches from the late '70s and early '80s reflect a certain lack of focus: while attempting to keep up with developments in the field he continued to teach, run the lab, and attend numerous conferences and conventions. Ironically, Stokoe's growing reputation resulted in the invitations that distracted him from the kind of in-depth investigation that had earned that reputation. One must remember that Stokoe worked on *Sign Language Structure* for three years and on the dictionary for five. Yet in the late 1970s and early 1980s he was delivering two or three addresses a month on topics as varied as "Gestural Signs in Codes and Languages," "Social Correlates of Sign Color Terms," "Language as a Foundation of Thought," and "Signing Apes and Evolving Linguistics." James Woodward puts it succinctly: "Some of Bill's work was extraordinarily innovative; some of it was not so innovative, and I think that's true of everybody's work. After a while even those people who constantly create, create smaller and smaller things. Bill's original discoveries made it possible for people to specialize. In the lab we were all focusing on one or two special topics — how could Bill know all about all of them?"[16]

Furthermore, Stokoe was spending more time publishing *Sign Language Studies* and directing Linstok Press (*lin* for linguistics, *stok* for Stokoe), the small publishing house that he had established with his inheritance. (When he named the press Stokoe also had in mind the old word *linstock*, meaning the staff that holds a lighted match for firing cannons. He chose the word to indicate that the press would set the world afire with ideas.) Stokoe wanted to use *Sign Language Studies* to share new information generated by his researchers and others in the field. He decided, he says, to leave the research to "the young, brilliant, well-trained scholars" and concentrate on disseminating their work:

> The lab and *Sign Language Studies* supported each other in a way. We had a great exchange of ideas with people from all over: Virginia Volterra from Italy, Brita Hansen from Denmark, Bernard Mottez from France, George Montgomery from Scotland — we had a continuing stream of researchers visiting us just to see what was going on in the lab. They would see what we were up to, and when they had a manuscript ready, they would send it to me for the journal. This kept me well enough supplied to be a successful editor.
>
> Subscriptions rose as people began to find out that we existed. By 1977 the work was so heavy I couldn't handle it myself since I was still working full-time at Gallaudet. I asked Ruth if she would like to do it, and in an office in the house, she filled the orders. By 1976 we were publishing a revision of the dictionary and of *Sign Language Structure*. Between books and the journal we kept quite busy.[17]

At about this time Stokoe purchased his first computer, an Apple II+, and a daisy-wheel printer. Within weeks he was facile enough to abandon the electric typewriter and produce camera-ready copy for *Sign Language Studies* "computer assisted." Keyboarding the entire contents of the journal took time, but he reasoned that he was combining editing with type composition.

Woodward and many others view *Sign Language Studies* as one of Stokoe's major contributions to the field of sign language research. During the 1970s some people accused Stokoe of publishing articles indiscriminately. However, as Woodward explains,

> This was a new field. Bill was anxious to get ideas out into circulation — in that way we could all respond to them, benefit from them. A lot would be lost waiting for "the perfect article." Bill was not impressed by such academic posturing.

Sign Language Studies enabled us to know everything that was going on in the field. Then we'd have the opportunity to decide for ourselves what was good and what was not so good. And we'd say, "Let's take this good stuff and do something with it; let's try to see what's wrong with the bad stuff." We wouldn't say, "Oh well, he or she doesn't know enough about this to support this study." Working with Bill and writing for *Sign Language Studies*, you never felt as if you were competing with anybody; you were making contributions to a body of knowledge.[18]

Editing, composing, and marketing the journal was in itself a full-time job, yet Stokoe continued to present papers at conferences, oversee the work of the lab, review scores of books and manuscripts, and serve as mentor to linguists and researchers from all over the world. Virginia Volterra remembers "constantly exchanging ideas and seeking his advice on problems and manuscripts I sent to him through our networks or through our meetings whenever I visited the States."[19]

Stokoe's primary concern, however, continued to be reaching as wide an audience as possible. According to Harry Markowicz, the crucial goal was, and still is,

to make sign language acceptable as a mode of communication for deaf adults in the community at large; and of greater importance for the welfare of the Deaf community, to make it acceptable as the medium for the educating of deaf children. In relation to this problem, psycholinguistic investigation of language acquisition will, it is to be hoped, shed light on how linguistic competence is established in an individual. This knowledge could then be applied to determine ways of educating deaf persons so that ultimately they can achieve true bilingualism: sign language competence for interpersonal communication in the Deaf community and linguistic competence . . . in written English, so that they can also partake of the common culture of the society in which they live.[20]

Bill Stokoe's focus hadn't changed at all since he first sat in a class at Gallaudet and observed the deaf students. In 1977, at a conference of the Niagara Linguistic Society, he reiterated the philosophy that originally had inspired his involvement in sign language. "The study of sign languages of the deaf has two chief ends," he declared: "to gain knowledge about what language is, and to help forward the education of deaf people." With great pride he claimed credit "for starting, or for helping on their way, several native signers [who became] qualified linguists and anthropologists."[21]

In 1977 Stokoe became eligible for a sabbatical. He and Ruth traveled to England, where he had been appointed a visiting fellow at Clare College, Cambridge University. There, Stokoe delivered an address entitled "Linguistics and Anthropology in Sign Language." In the speech he added historical and cultural perspectives to his linguistic findings to further justify the recognition and use of sign language. "Knowledge about human societies and their languages was blocked for a long time by our Western inability to see beyond our own several languages," he observed, concluding with the admonition that "blindness to sign languages in the twentieth century will look as ridiculous now as was deafness to Chaucer's English or Dante's Italian six hundred years ago."[22]

The Stokoes were given an apartment on Scholar's Walk, and they dined in the common room with "people from all branches of academia." Stokoe remembers that "there was a good bar there, a good coffee machine, and great conversation." As always, he and Ruth were happiest when traveling together. It was their third trip to Europe, and they were getting to know England well enough to feel at home there.

But the travel, the good conversation, the absence of politics "made it even harder" for Stokoe to return to Gallaudet, where "the president and his six vice presidents would meet and set college policy without consulting the faculty." While Stokoe was on sabbatical the administration had adopted a resolution whereby all signing and interpreting at Gallaudet would be performed in "Sim Com," or simultaneous communication (the speaker of Sim Com talks and signs simultaneously). Stokoe "wrote letters to the administration" in protest, "but it was butting my head against a soft belly."[23]

It was as if all the research supporting American Sign Language had never occurred. Dennis Cokely recollects that a study completed in 1979 by Marmor and Pettito had shown clearly the inadequacy of Sim Com. Marmor and Pettito concluded that, "given the difficulty that most hearing people encounter in trying to use simultaneous communication, it is not surprising that . . . there is a great deal of deletion and miscommunication which occurs among users of these artificial codes."[24]

At about the time Gallaudet adopted Sim Com, Stokoe delivered a lecture in Newcastle, England, explaining the disadvantages of Sim Com and the advantages of "actual sign language discourse" (ASL). In the lecture he described an application of ASL he had seen recently at the first National Symposium on Sign Language Research and Teaching, held in Chicago:

> Instead of simultaneous interpretation — which is, after all, only the representation of the English being spoken [with] surrogates for words — the participants saw, in Lou Fant's virtuoso presentation, and many understood, actual sign language discourse in formal authentic style. Moreover, the alternating presentation, first in Sign and then in English, freed both languages from the constraint of trying for simultaneity, so that the presenter's literary style in both languages could be appreciated. Thus we saw something more than a series of speakers saying that Sign was the language of the deaf and deserved respect. We saw the language in actual use; we saw the deaf participants glowing with deserved gratification — no longer the second-class citizens at a convention of pedantic talkers but the respected and appreciated possessors of a language that the hearing participants were humbly striving to learn more about. . . .
>
> Many of us are well aware that the meeting represented the state of the art in the study of sign languages; the state of the art of utilizing what we know about Sign in schools and classes for the deaf is another matter. . . . Few school executives will even allow any talk about the use of American Sign Language in their classrooms and dormitories and grounds. Even new graduate students in linguistics who have not yet experienced the full heat of anti-Sign opposition or the dull, plodding blindness to Sign of the less militant, more easygoing older teachers know full well that American Sign Language is still

a threatened species of language, if only because of their own difficulty in finding suitable informants, in getting credit for their sign language as a working language in graduate studies, and in getting academic encouragement and support for their study of a still largely unrecognized language.[25]

It was business as usual when Stokoe returned from sabbatical. His fame had spread throughout the world, but in the world's only liberal arts college for the deaf his findings were still ignored.

By 1979 Stokoe's work had begun to attract favorable attention in the popular press. The *Washington Post* published a two-page article about him together with a particularly striking photograph, in which Stokoe signs while standing before the enormous bronze sculpture of T. H. Gallaudet opposite Chapel Hall on the Gallaudet campus. The sculpture represents Gallaudet teaching Alice Cogswell how to sign the letter *A*. The symbolism couldn't be more fitting: It was T. H. Gallaudet who brought the use of sign language for instruction to America, and it was Bill Stokoe who would bring it back again to occupy its rightful place in the education of deaf people.

Stokoe was also becoming better known among deaf professionals in fields other than ASL research, such as education and the legal rights of deaf people. Many of these people were graduates of Gallaudet and had known Stokoe there. They met him at conferences and workshops, visited his lab, and corresponded with him; he published their papers in *Sign Language Studies*. The original skepticism among deaf people toward a hearing man's "examining" their method of communication had given way to respect and appreciation for his scholarship and for the recognition he brought to their language. As Merv Garretson says, "We were all surprised by it; [we] never thought it would amount to anything. Now he's a folk hero."[26] Harlan Lane equates Bill Stokoe's influence in the United States with that of the nineteenth-century Frenchman R. A. Bebian, a friend of Laurent Clerc, who "had great admiration for deaf people and their language, recognized their oppression, and labored mightily, in part through books, articles, and a journal he edited, to improve the appreciation of deaf language and culture."[27]

Stokoe's influence has been so profound that to discuss American Sign Language without mentioning his findings is virtually impossible. As Harlan Lane explains:

> Stokoe's work and that of Klima and Bellugi are the pillars on which the whole scholarly edifice was erected. His papers laid the intellectual groundwork. His dictionary presented some of the first evidence that persuaded linguists that natural language could come out of the hands instead of the tongue. The students and postdoctoral fellows he trained went on to create with him the literature of ASL linguistics and psycholinguistics, which in turn was the basis for the present cultural renaissance of the American Deaf community.[28]

In 1980 Stokoe's friends in the lab decided to plan a celebration of his work, not only to honor his monumental achievements but to offset the indifference and outright animosity he still faced at Gallaudet (where support for Sim Com continued despite his protests). Baker-Shenk and Battison decided to honor Stokoe with a collection of essays, to be presented to him at the 1980 convention of the National Association of the Deaf. That year's convention was particularly important because it marked the association's 100th anniversary. In the introduction to the book of essays, entitled *Sign Language and the Deaf Community*, Baker-Shenk explains how the book came to be and why:

> In July of 1979 we sent out a letter to fifteen individuals, asking them to contribute to a Festschrift in honor of Bill Stokoe. Each of these individuals had worked with Dr. Stokoe or had been influenced by his work, and all were actively involved as professionals in research, teaching, or other uses of sign language. We told them we wanted to describe the impact of sign language research on the Deaf community, and we asked each of them to write a paper that would trace the historical development of their professional fields as well as to describe their own involvement in those fields and their personal and professional interactions with Dr. Stokoe.

This volume is, collectively, a "labor of love" — a tribute to a man who stubbornly continued his pioneering work on American Sign Language despite considerable political obstacles, public scorn, and little support from his colleagues. Now all of us are reaping the benefits of his determination and perseverance, and the world itself has begun to recognize the truth of his "shocking" claim that American Sign Language is a language worthy of full recognition, study, and use — on a par with all other languages of the world.

During the past ten years, this recognition of American Sign Language has had an increasing impact on the traditionally negative attitudes of professionals who interact with Deaf people — educators, teachers, interpreters, audiologists, therapists, and others. No longer are these professionals able to view Deaf people as "defective hearing people." With the recognition that Deaf people use a highly complex language that is elegantly structured to fit the capabilities of the signer's eyes and body comes the recognition that having a hearing loss means interacting in a *different* way, but by no means an inferior way. This new understanding of American Sign Language enables us to see that Deaf people have their own culture and values that are expressed in this language — and that the culture, its values, and its language deserve the respect of all individuals who interact professionally and personally with Deaf people.[29]

The Festschrift essays themselves, published by the National Association of the Deaf, reflect many of the changes that have occurred in large part as a result of Stokoe's work. The word "deaf" is printed in lowercase to describe people with a hearing loss but capitalized when it describes people who form a society or culture. The contributors include leading researchers in the field of sign language, ten of whom have worked with Stokoe in the lab, and three Europeans — another reflection of the extent of Stokoe's influence. All of the contributors agreed to donate their royalties to a scholarship fund to be set up in Bill Stokoe's name and administered by the National Association of the Deaf. The funds have been used every year since 1979 to support a

deaf student at the graduate or undergraduate level who is interested in doing research in sign language or deaf communication.

Bill Stokoe knew nothing about the approaching celebration.
Baker-Shenk recalls the plan to lure him onstage for a surprise
presentation of the Festschrift. She told him, "We're going to
give an award to someone, and since you're Bill Stokoe, it would
mean so much if you would present it to him. Just hand it to him.
You don't have to say anything." She explained to him that she
would appear with him onstage, along with Gil Eastman, Ralph
White (president of the National Association of the Deaf), and
Dennis Cokely. Stokoe "was so used to being an honorary figure
that he didn't even ask me questions," she says. "He just told me
to tell him what to do and when to do it."

When the time came the five of them were sitting in a row
onstage, facing more than two thousand people in the ballroom.
"The first person got up," Baker-Shenk recalls,

> and started talking about the history of the deaf and of Amer-
> ican Sign Language. Then the next person got up and added
> to it. It was all rehearsed, of course. We had talked about it
> and planned who was going to say what very carefully. I was
> the speaker directly before Bill.
>
> Now, by this time he was standing right next to me and
> holding the box I had given him. He was starting to look
> around a little bit, wondering why no one was left onstage to
> whom he would give this thing. But it still didn't click. As I
> spoke, I began to narrow my comments down more and
> more, talking about this man who had done such and such a
> thing, until finally it became clear that I could only be speak-
> ing about one person. Bill started to look down at the box,
> then he looked around rather helplessly, then he looked at
> the box again. It was a funny, wonderful moment. I finally
> said that the man we were talking about, the man we had
> gathered to honor, was William C. Stokoe. At that point, Bill
> bent over ever so slightly; he told me later that his knees
> almost gave way and he was trying not to fall over. When he
> opened the box, he found the book, *Sign Language and the
> Deaf Community*, with his picture [reprinted from the *Wash-
> ington Post* article] and his name on the cover. He stood there

holding it, just sort of showing it to everybody, and the audience gave him a long, thunderous, standing ovation. This was only one of the many honors that Bill received, but it was a very special one because it came from people who knew his work and it was witnessed by people who had benefitted from his work.[30]

It was a very special time. Ruth Stokoe had written an essay for the book and helped choose the photographs. She had also helped Baker-Shenk and Battison with the preparations, and Bill remembers her relief that he had not learned about the surprise in advance.

Gil Eastman also remembers the occasion well, including a conversation with Stokoe the day after the presentation:

> I was walking in the hallway of the hotel, and I saw Bill coming toward me, looking as if he were in a daze. I said, "Hey Bill, how are you?" I thought he was still in shock over the award. He said, "Oh, I feel great, I feel for the first time as if I'm in the world of the deaf, and it's fascinating." He told me that he had gone to a lot of conventions in linguistics, English, and so on, but this was the first time he had ever gone to a convention where so many deaf people had attended, and he noticed something different. I asked him what it was. He said that he realized for the first time that when deaf people come together and see one another, they say, "Hello, haven't seen you in a long time," then they give each other hugs. That hugging really impressed him, even perhaps more than the award. I'm telling you, that's Deaf culture, and although Bill was an expert on the language of the deaf, he was just beginning to realize, to see for himself, our specialness, our uniqueness.[31]

Eastman's recollection of Stokoe's "first" experience with deaf culture is particularly telling. Stokoe had been working with deaf students and, as his research expanded, with deaf informants and researchers for more than twenty-five years — yet he had just discovered something very fundamental about the way deaf people interact with each other. This says more about deaf culture than it does about Bill Stokoe. He was a warm and friendly man; he had scores of deaf friends and had observed them in many and various situations. Furthermore, the fact that the National Association of the Deaf had chosen to honor him is testimony to the respect and gratitude deaf people felt for him.

However, as a hearing man he had never actually gotten *inside* deaf culture. An explanation for this can be found in an essay by Barbara Kannapell entitled "Inside the Deaf Community." Kannapell explains the relationships that form among deaf people — relationships that almost inevitably exclude hearing people — as follows:

> Deaf people experience a strong bond of communication because they have common topics to share which are based on common experiences, such as the history of deaf people, school experiences, family experiences, sports, movies, stories, and jokes. They develop strong relationships based on these common experiences with other deaf people. Many deaf people develop strong relationships during school years and maintain these relationships throughout their lives. This feeling may be carried over from residential schools, where they developed a strong bond of communication for the purpose of survival.
>
> If a deaf person behaves like a hearing person, other deaf people will sign "hearing" on the forehead to show that "he thinks like a hearing person." Thus, he is on the fringe of the Deaf community, depending on his attitudes. Conversely, if a hearing person behaves like a deaf person, other deaf people may sign "strong deaf" or "fluent ASL," which means that the person is culturally deaf. Thus, he or she is admitted to the core of the Deaf community.[32]

In 1990 Stokoe said he still felt there was a language barrier between him and deaf people. "I don't really have the kind of proficiency in American Sign Language that would make me feel comfortable as part of a group," he explained. "On rare occasions when I'm with a group of deaf people I know, I can enter into it and shed some of my English-speaking traits and sign a little bit more ASL-like, but I'll never penetrate to the real center."[33]

The fact that Bill Stokoe — the man who proved deaf people

have a sophisticated language and culture of their own — cannot "penetrate to the real center" is explainable in part by the discoveries he made. American Sign Language is the legitimate language of a cultural minority. By "legitimizing" their language, Stokoe, in some sense, gave the deaf minority the power to decide who is and who is not a member. This is not to say that deaf people were unaware that they had a language and culture before Bill Stokoe published the results of his research. But no one before Stokoe had conducted scientific studies to validate that fact and show the world that ASL was a language worthy of examination and respect.

The observation Stokoe shared with Gil Eastman in the hotel hallway was just that — an observation. As a researcher whose lifelong interest was the language used by deaf people, it was fascinating for Stokoe to make this new discovery about the way deaf people interacted. And of course he was sincere in writing, around the same time, that as an "outsider" he was "humbly grateful for the hospitality and shared wisdom" shown to him by deaf people.[34] However, to be considered a member of deaf culture was not necessary to his personal happiness or his professional success.

Stokoe's life, in fact, was based very much in the hearing world. Although he had not taught literature for many years, he could recite verse after verse of his favorite British poets; he loved riddles, puns, and plays on words — all of which translated poorly when he tried to share them with deaf people. He played the bagpipes and loved Scottish music; he loved English pub songs.

Bill Stokoe's discoveries led deaf people to a new level of empowerment. Even if that empowerment had resulted eventually in his being excluded from further research or participation in the deaf community (something that most certainly did not happen), he would have derived satisfaction from his achievement.

But for hearing parents afraid of losing the ability to interact fully with their deaf children and for many teachers not fluent in American Sign Language, it was hard to view the situation with equanimity. For them, Bill Stokoe and the Linguistics Research Lab were rocking a very large boat. Many hearing people continued to advocate what James Woodward describes as "a combined method of speech and signs that parallel English word order."[35] The findings of the LRL could not have pleased these people. Citing Markowicz and Padden, Woodward explains why the boat needed to be rocked:

Most Deaf children have not received meaningful Deaf cultural input from teachers or family, since teachers and families are mostly Hearing. Authoritarian language oppression can very easily occur under these situations. As we have already seen, the schools have tended to repress sign language, especially ASL, and input from deaf adults; and . . . even those that permit sign language discriminate against ASL, the language varieties that Deaf people normally identify with. Other minority group children often have a refuge in the home from such cultural and linguistic oppression. However, as we have seen, more than 90 percent of Deaf children who attended residential schools do not have parents who belong to the same minority group as they do. Thus Deaf children are much less protected from cultural and linguistic discrimination than children from other minority groups.[36]

Worldwide recognition such as that which Stokoe received at the 1980 convention of the National Association of the Deaf was in large part responsible for the continued functioning of the LRL. At Gallaudet manual English, Cued Speech, and Simultaneous Communication continued to be advocated for the classroom in preference to American Sign Language. Bill Stokoe remembers that "every time I sat down with the vice president for research and the dean of research, they asked me when I was going to retire."[37] It was becoming clear to Stokoe that the administration at Gallaudet would never make life easy for him and his researchers. He recalls, for example, that

During the later years in the lab, when it was just me, Dennis [Cokely], Charlotte [Baker-Shenk], a secretary, and a couple of part-time people, I had to submit annual reviews of our work. After I submitted them, I'd get feedback from the administrators saying that I should sit harder on my associates Baker-Shenk and Cokely because they weren't really researchers, they were playing an advocacy rather than a research and scientific role. The administrators said we weren't doing real research. But what we weren't doing was the kind of psychological testing that maintained the status quo — we were not contributing to the attitudes, the ignorance, the arrogance and power of the people who had been in control of deaf education for so long — so we weren't too popular on campus.[38]

By the mid-1970s George Detmold had retired and moved to Florida, "far away from the politics and the problems." But he and Stokoe maintained their close friendship and corresponded often. Detmold remembers that during the early 1980s the administration "really started sticking it to Bill. No one else would have been able to stand it as long as he did."[39]

On one occasion the administration refused Stokoe travel money for an international conference in Germany although he had been invited to deliver the keynote address. He was told he hadn't completed the proper forms. On another occasion, Stokoe was told that his pay would be reduced because his status had changed from "faculty" to "administrative." Only when Stokoe threatened to complain to the American Association of University Professors was the change rescinded.

The adversarial atmosphere that permeated most of Bill Stokoe's dealings at Gallaudet was taking its toll. When Stokoe began his research, he did so with the blessing of his best friend, George Detmold. The college had been small then and decisions could be reached without wading through bureaucratic levels of approvals and appropriations. Gallaudet had changed considerably from those early days, and the "bureaucrats" were in charge. Gallaudet was a large, government-funded institution with rules, regulations, and policies that had been instituted by elected committees and approved by an academic senate. The era when one person such as George Detmold could make the decision to assign funds to a lab or department was long gone. In Stokoe's view, the bureaucrats wanted to close his lab because the research produced there subverted their efforts to maintain the status quo — and in maintaining the status quo they were undermining the education of deaf students.

In the view of these administrators, however, Stokoe's lab had been created primarily to find a place for a tenured English professor. And that tenured professor harped continually on the foolishness of their administrative and management styles and their pedagogical philosophies. Standing up for his principles, as always, Stokoe criticized these people at every opportunity; in return, they asked him at every opportunity when he was going to retire.

Beginning in March of 1982, Stokoe helped his friend Virginia Volterra of the Institute of Psychology in Rome to plan the Third International Symposium on Sign Language Research, to be held in Rome in June of 1983. There was nothing that he would have preferred to do, and there was no one who could do it better, given his energy, his commitment, his contacts, and his knowledge of the field. He and Volterra began an exchange of notes by airmail. Volterra has saved the notebooks because, as she explains,

> They are so important to my scientific life. They are really a record of a part of my education. My English was not good; it is still not good, but Bill Stokoe never cared about that. I started to discuss with him through this notebook sign language research in general, and my research. I could explain to him what I had in mind and he answered me, gave me suggestions, told me if an idea was good or not, how I could develop it, what was going on in the States.
>
> When the first notebook was filled, we started a second one, which we used until after the conference. Just recently we started to send disks back and forth. . . . This has been an incredible experience, to have an exchange of ideas with a person like Bill Stokoe. We have great respect for Bill Stokoe in Italy.[40]

The notebooks covered everything related to the conference, and more: the topics to be addressed; the design of the invitations (a rendering by a deaf Italian girl of the Coliseum with four columns drawn as hands fingerspelling the word "R O M E"); when invitations should be sent; the source of funding for interpreters; the reaction to a lecture by Baker-Shenk in Italy in June of 1982 ("tell her the people at the institute were very impressed — one of the best they have listened to. Tell her how much "bravo" she was!").

But politics were always present. On July 6, 1982, Stokoe used the notebook to complain:

I got very impatient with Dr. Merrill and his stooge (what's the Italian word for stooge?) trying to pick out who will go from Gallaudet to *your* symposium.

They tried that at the time of the International Conference of Educators of the Deaf in Hamburg. I got very angry and expostulated in person and in memos, and they caved in — I had been asked by one of the Germans to do a paper on ASL. Later, Merrill came up with a scheme in which anyone who wanted to represent Gallaudet had to submit an abstract to them.

Finally, I decided not to go to Germany anyway. I did that because when I saw the program, it was all oralism, speech therapy, audiology, and treating deaf people like medical patients. But I'm sure Dr. Merrill still thinks it was because he was so stuffy about the travel money. Of course, he and selected members of the administration hop off to Japan, Australia, etc., to visit schools any time they like.

There is no moral to this story, but it has a happy ending: E. C. Merrill has announced his intention to resign next year![41]

But the ending wasn't so happy after all. The conference in Rome was a huge success, with the most prominent researchers in the world presenting papers, including many people who had worked with Stokoe. However, Merrill's departure did not put an end to Stokoe's problems with the Gallaudet administration.

When Stokoe returned to the United States, pressure mounted anew to force him into retirement and replace the lab with a Department of Linguistics that would "streamline" Gallaudet's research projects. This time around, intrigue flavored the political brew. In 1983 Merrill was replaced as president of Gallaudet by Dr. W. Lloyd Johns. But by January of 1984, Johns's personal life had become the subject of gossip, both on and off campus. He wrote a memo to the Gallaudet community announcing that he and his wife had legally separated, that she had moved to California, and that this disruption would "in no way deter Gallaudet from the achievements and potential all of us recognize and desire."[42] However, the issue was too embarrassing, too well known, to be contained, and in the summer of 1984 Johns was forced to resign as president and was replaced by Jerry C. Lee.

None of this would have influenced Stokoe's plans, if not for unfortunate timing. In the early summer of 1983, Stokoe decided to retire in August of 1984, after thirty-nine years at Gallaudet. "I stayed as long as I did," he says, "primarily for the crass motive of building up my retirement benefits."[43] But he had another reason as well. Cokely's and Baker-Shenk's research in the LRL was crucial to the completion of their dissertations, and Stokoe feared that if he left before they finished and the lab closed, they would be unable to complete their work elsewhere. He believed that once they had their doctorates, they would be considered qualified to continue their work in the lab or to work elsewhere on campus.

The Gallaudet administration wasted no time. In 1983, as soon as Bill announced his decision to retire in 1984, the administration announced its intention to close the lab. Stokoe, Baker-Shenk, and Cokely immediately began a letter-writing campaign, asking almost every linguist in the world concerned with sign language research to write to the new president, Dr. Johns. The response was overwhelming. More than fifty letters arrived from thirty-five states and from countries all over the world — Sweden, Italy, Canada, Thailand, Japan, Denmark, Switzerland, Scotland, and England. The letter-writers, some of the best known researchers, writers, and educators in the field, expressed incredulity at the idea of closing the world's preeminent lab for sign language research.

Jerome Schein, who was by this time a professor and director of deafness rehabilitation at New York University, wrote to President Johns. He wrote to Bill Stokoe as well, expressing the hope that "these few words convey the entirety of my willingness to support you. You and your research colleagues are the cutting edge in expanding our understanding of deafness."[44]

Ursula Bellugi wrote to Johns, saying, "It is dramatically clear that the scientific world recognizes the critical role that the Linguistics Research Laboratory has held in developing an understanding of human language; [therefore] it seems to me that it is timely for Gallaudet College also to acknowledge and support the Linguistics Research Laboratory, its important contributions, and its future studies."[45]

François Grosjean, coauthor with Harlan Lane of *Recent Perspectives on American Sign Language*, wrote from Switzerland to report that he had heard

> some very distressing news. I cannot but address myself to you to give you my reaction and that of the sign language linguists here in Europe.
>
> Being acquainted with both the European and American academic worlds, I know how easy it is back in the States to take certain accomplishments for granted and to neglect their impact on the world community. Dr. Stokoe's accomplishments as well as those of his team have that world impact. In a Europe that is finally awakening to the language and culture of its deaf communities, the research that is done in the Linguistics Research Laboratory is seen as an example to follow and a beacon of hope. Whenever I give a lecture on sign language research, I am asked questions about Gallaudet and its research on ASL. . . . The very reputation of Gallaudet as a college, here in Europe, is based in large part on Dr. Stokoe's laboratory, and that is why no one here can understand why there is talk of closing it down.
>
> I would like to end on a more personal note. My own work on the psycholinguistics of sign language has been greatly influenced by the research done in the Linguistics Research Laboratory. I admire the work of Dr. Stokoe, Charlotte Baker-Shenk, and Dennis Cokely and believe it is of great importance, both for our knowledge of sign language and for the deaf community. As a researcher in the field, I ask you therefore to do everything in your power to maintain the Linguistics Research Laboratory and to retain and promote the researchers that work in it.[46]

The anthropologist Gordon Hewes wrote from the University of Colorado that "researchers and investigators in several fields have come to depend on the steady flow of important papers from the Gallaudet LRL."[47]

Harlan Lane reminded President Johns of Stokoe's worldwide reputation:

I am informed that some of the activities in language science
for which Gallaudet College has been so rightly renowned
are in jeopardy; it would be remiss of a friend of the college
not to speak up if this were the case. I feel I qualify for that
title as I have long been an interested student of developments at Gallaudet, and was honored with the offer of the
deanship of the College of Communications a few years ago.

In the unanimous view of scholars of language in general
and of sign language in particular who are familiar with the
work of your Linguistics Research Laboratory over the past
two decades, it has made an extremely valuable contribution
to our understanding of the nature of language and its biological basis, to a description of American and other sign
languages, and to progress in teaching and translating American Sign Language. It is not an exaggeration to say that the
nationwide renaissance of scholarly and lay interest in sign
occurred because of the foundations laid by William Stokoe
and collaborators such as Charlotte Baker-Shenk and Dennis
Cokely. While I served on the Linguistics Panel of the National Science Foundation, I had several opportunities to
study research proposals from this laboratory: they were
marked by sophistication, circumspection, and cogency.
Moreover, virtually every proposal we received concerning
sign language — and we received more than in any other
single specialty — cited the work of Dr. Stokoe and his
collaborators.

If there is indeed a basis for the perception that the work of
these and allied scholars is not receiving the full support of
your administration, I urge you to seek an independent evaluation by outside scholars and practitioners. There can be few
programs at your school, sir, that are more deserving of your
support, that of the college, and of the deaf community.[48]

President Johns was concerned enough to reply to each letter, stating with bureaucratic finesse: "I have not been informed
of any plan or program to reduce or eliminate the research area
you identify, but I will review the matter."[49]

Had Johns remained at Gallaudet, it seems likely he would have chosen to appease the linguistic community. However, the impact of the many letters from around the world was lost the moment he announced his resignation. There was no time for Stokoe, whose retirement date had arrived, to mount another letter-writing campaign directed at the next new president.

In November of 1984, three months after Jerry Lee took over the presidency of Gallaudet, *On The Green* (the weekly newspaper for Gallaudet faculty and staff) announced that the Linguistics Research Lab would close at the end of December. Readers were assured that

> The closing of the lab does not reflect a change in the college's commitment to study language. Research will continue to be conducted throughout the campus. Since the inception of the lab, the college has established the Department of Linguistics, the Department of Sign Communication, and the Department of Interpreter/Transliterator Instruction — each of which is involved in sign language research. In addition, other units of the Research Institute have started to conduct research on sign language," Trybus [dean of the Gallaudet Research Institute] stated.
>
> Direction this fall by Gallaudet president Jerry C. Lee to broaden the scope of research and redirect funds to new kinds of research forced the institute to "rethink and reexamine" its work, Trybus said. "We felt we could safely discontinue the laboratory and not endanger the research since it is permeated throughout campus. It is no longer necessary to have a separate lab conducting the research.[50]

The administrators and faculty at Gallaudet made no attempt to save the lab, in part because Stokoe had made many enemies along the way but, more important, because they hadn't liked what he was doing. Almost twenty years after the publication of *Sign Language Structure*, the administration and most of the faculty at Gallaudet still hadn't figured out why they, the majority, should try to learn this minority language, much less accord its users respect and autonomy.

The administrators had rehearsed their lines well. Their diplomatic remarks were reported in the student newspaper, the

Buff and Blue: "Dr. Stokoe's work will continue at Gallaudet, only in different ways." . . . "Other departments and people are doing sign language research." . . . "We can close that small group of researchers without hurting sign language." . . . "We had to change something." . . . "The members of the Linguistics Department are all respected, competent researchers and all are supportive of ASL."[51]

The administrators really did protest too much, and the students at Gallaudet knew it. The *Buff and Blue* article critical of the decision to close the "world-famous" LRL, observed that

> The departments cited by Trybus as doing sign language research include the Department of Linguistics, the Center for Education and Human Development, the Department of Interpreter/Transliterator Instruction, the Department of Sign Communication, the Office of Assessment and Demographic Studies. In addition, Dr. James Woodward, a noted sociolinguist, is working part-time for GRI [Gallaudet Research Institute]. However, apart from the Department of Linguistics, which is doing a project on "Predictive Factors in Reading," and the Center for Education and Human Development, which is doing a joint study with the Department of Linguistics on "Sign Variations in Context," and Dr. Woodward's part-time research, there is no evidence that the other departments mentioned by Dr. Trybus are, in fact, doing ASL linguistics research.
>
> It is important to note that since 1971, Stokoe's work was done on a full-time basis by trained linguists or those in training to become linguists in the LRL. With the exception of the three linguists in the Linguistics Department, who are expected to teach 80 percent of their time with 20 percent going to research, and Dr. Woodward, who lives and works in California, none of the people expected by Dr. Trybus to carry on Dr. Stokoe's work are trained linguists.
>
> Additionally, the two world-renowned ASL linguists now working full-time for the LRL, Dennis Cokely and Dr. Charlotte Baker-Shenk, coauthors of the widely used series of texts titled *American Sign Language*, will no longer be em-

ployed by this college in any capacity after December 31, 1984.

When asked why Baker-Shenk and Cokely were not transferred to the Linguistics Department, Dr. Schuchman said, "Three linguistic faculty members are enough."

Dr. Trybus, commenting on the dismissal of Cokely and Baker-Shenk said, "When you need to change the direction of a program, it means you need different skills."[52]

Charlotte Baker-Shenk believes that closing the lab was, "in a sense, an intelligent thing to do." The LRL researchers

were beginning to chip away at the administrators' power, so it was a wise decision on their part to get rid of us. It was politically and strategically a necessary thing to do if they wanted to maintain things the way they had been. We were becoming more powerful. The ASL movement was beginning to really take hold. Even though not a lot of change was happening at Gallaudet, a lot was beginning to happen in other places. Our ability to articulate the implications of our research was improving, and that's when it got really scary for them. We started spending a lot of time doing that. That's when we began to be labeled as biased, as going beyond the appropriate behavior for researchers.

To me the argument about scientific objectivity is a myth. It was so clear to us that as long as we did research the way the majority of them did it and came out with their kind of results, that was called being objective. But for us, what they were doing was based on false assumptions about the language and the culture of the deaf community. Therefore, the methodology was flawed and the results didn't make any sense. So instead we were saying, "Here are our assumptions based on research: that deaf people have a different language, they have a different culture, and therefore we shape our research or methodology in this form based on those assumptions."

Our results were very different from their results because our assumptions to begin with were very different, as were our methodologies, not just in terms of qualitative versus quantitative research. We knew we needed to work with confederates, that is, bridge people who knew the language and the culture. We knew that without bridge people we could not get authentic, reliable results because of all the code switching that would happen when a deaf person interacted with us. It was such a polarized environment, an environment where deaf people had been oppressed for so many years, you could not expect them suddenly to show you their language and behavior as they normally would with each other when no hearing people were present.

So we began to work with bridge people who were bicultural in order to get some results that reflected what deaf people really did. But the researchers from "the other side" would only accept their own findings, which fit their assumption that deaf people were like defective hearing people. They could use the same instruments and procedures they always had and think that they were getting an accurate reading of the abilities and the ways of thinking of deaf people.[53]

Even before President Johns left, Doin Hicks, the vice president for research, decided that he had to deal with the "outside opinions" expressed in the letter-writing campaign. He wrote to Raymond Trybus to inform him that

The actions of Bill Stokoe in generating the "fan letters" addressed to Dr. Johns by a variety of individuals both in the United States and elsewhere are entirely inappropriate and represent, in my view, nothing short of serious insubordination. This is so because the tone of many of the letters makes it quite clear that they were written in response to specific, inaccurate, and apparently inflammatory statements made by Stokoe (and/or his LRL colleagues) regarding you and me and our intentions, statements, and actions regarding his program.[54]

There was nothing inaccurate about the statements of Stokoe and his LRL colleagues. Hicks and Trybus wanted the lab closed and Baker-Shenk and Cokely out of Gallaudet. They were furious at Stokoe for presuming, as Hicks put it, to "'declare independence' from the normal review and administrative processes of the Research Institute and Division of Research — this, of course, has been one of the major problems with which we have been struggling for the last year or two with this group."[55]

The problem wasn't simply Bill Stokoe's insubordination: it was what he represented. The letters of support came not only from linguists but from deaf students who had "been helped personally and professionally" by the work of Bill Stokoe;[56] from Barbara Kannapell, founder of DeafPride, who credited Bill and his lab with "contributing to the positive self-image of deaf people";[57] from Anne Fadiman, a writer for *Life* magazine who had met Stokoe while researching an article at Gallaudet and discovered the beauty of American Sign Language.[58] Stokoe's work had produced a revolution. From the point of view of Gallaudet's administrators, the sooner they could get rid of him the better.

Carol Padden, who today is one of several deaf members of the Board of Trustees at Gallaudet, recently observed that

> Gallaudet, sad to say, has lost many opportunities to bring prestige to itself, including nurturing Bill and using his work and his leadership for Gallaudet's advantage. Gallaudet has never been very good at distinguishing between ill-conceived experiments (e.g., Cued Speech, Signing Exact English) and true scholarship. Now, I think Gallaudet is happy to recognize Bill, but it is a recognition that has come far too late. And I still think it is too little. They should name a building after him at the very least.[59]

Charlotte Baker-Shenk remembers that when Bill Stokoe retired, he was "a tired man, tired of all the fighting, tired of all the meetings and tired of having to go to battle all the time. He kept the wolves at bay for Dennis and me. And that letter-writing campaign was exhausting, but he did it for us, and for the lab, and for what he believed in. But when he retired, I think he believed that he had somehow failed."[60]

A month or two after the closing of the lab, Virginia Covington went over to the new Department of Linguistics to locate something that had been in the library of the lab, a collection Stokoe had organized and labeled himself, which Baker-Shenk has described as "one of the most complete collections of sign language linguistics material in the world."[61] As Covington recalls, "I went over there . . . and introduced myself and said that I was wondering what happened to Bill's materials. They just looked at me blankly, then pointed to a corner and said, "That must be what those boxes are." They had just thrown this tremendous linguistic library — articles, beautifully organized and filed, anything you wanted — into boxes and stacked them in a corner. They didn't seem to care. To them it was junk and they didn't know what to do with it."[62]

That's not surprising. They had never known what to do with Bill Stokoe, either.

CHAPTER 8

· · · · · · ·

If there is a place where unconscious signifying and communicating come together with the conscious use of language, it is in the realm of signs made with human bodies and read with human vision.

WILLIAM STOKOE

The Linguistics Research Laboratory closed, but Stokoe's letter-writing campaign had a lasting effect. Today, more than ten
years later, the administration at Gallaudet is still criticized for
its actions. I. King Jordan says the school's reputation has not
recovered.

> Bill should have brought great prestige to Gallaudet, but the
> administration, in its "wisdom," closed down the Linguistics
> Research Lab. Now that I'm president I'm not sure how to go
> about explaining why that happened. It has caused me a lot of
> headaches, because the message that the world received . . .
> was that we were devaluing American Sign Language. The
> response of the administration was, "No, no, there's a De-
> partment of Linguistics and there are other units on campus
> that do the same research."
>
> But I don't care how many times or how forcefully you say
> something like that, people say "That's nonsense." It still
> hurts us today. People still ask, "Why did Gallaudet ever
> close down the Linguistics Research Lab?" People all over
> the world who know about the study of American Sign Lan-
> guage know Bill Stokoe's name.[1]

When Stokoe retired at the end of 1984, he was sixty-five and
Ruth Stokoe was sixty-four. They were comfortable enough on
Bill's pension and Social Security to continue to travel occasionally. They "settled down in retirement," Stokoe says, in the
same house they had bought in 1957, but much improved by
Stokoe's tinkering, "with Ruth continuing to conduct her National Gallery tours, and I editing the journal and seeing the
children and grandchildren and friends, and going out to things
occasionally — a very quiet but satisfying life together."[2]

Ruth had never liked riding on her husband's motorcycle,
but their granddaughter, Jennifer, was a regular passenger
whenever she visited. And the mild success of Linstok Press
allowed Bill to indulge his passion for computers, installing all
the latest software and keeping abreast of technological developments that would make the journal more readable and easier
to manage.

It never occurred to Stokoe to abandon his work after retirement. He continues to lecture and to write and review books.

Sign Language Studies has improved with age: As more people have become aware of its existence and submitted articles, Stokoe has been able to publish more selectively. But he has never lost sight of the journal's purpose. *Sign Language Studies* is one of the few scholarly journals dealing with a range of topics of concern to deaf people. It addresses not only linguistic but educational, sociological, and anthropological issues. Tom Humphries, coauthor of *Deaf in America* and a frequent contributor to *Sign Language Studies*, says it is

> one of the few journals I read from cover to cover these days. I don't think there is any greater collection of articles related to sign language and deaf culture in any journal anywhere. I like the fact that it doesn't have to be a journal of linguistic inquiry all the time and accepts articles on social structure and education issues. Its main contribution, I think, is that it is a place to print good articles that might not get published anywhere else for a variety of reasons. It also offers a context of serious works in which to publish such articles.[3]

I. King Jordan "can't imagine not reading" *Sign Language Studies:*

> It is such an important publication. It's the only journal there is that focuses exclusively on the study of sign language and the people who use it. I think that maybe one of the most important things about it is that there is a lot of writing in it about deaf culture and deaf community. It shows, with each issue, that Bill's definition of American Sign Language is the same kind of definition that one would have of any language.[4]

Harlan Lane, who received a John D. and Catherine T. MacArthur Foundation Fellowship in 1991 for his work on deaf culture and language, offers high praise for *Sign Language Studies:* "What a remarkable achievement it is. In connection with writing a book I have just finished, I recently had occasion to line up all the issues on my shelf and read them through from beginning to end; I found many old friends, seminal papers, and a richness of texture — language, culture, anthropology, sociology, psychology — that few journals could rival."[5]

Stokoe recalls that he and Ruth enjoyed working on *Sign Language Studies* together after his retirement.

Ruth double-checked everything, her own work as well as mine — maybe triple-checked. So we complemented each other. I was the adventurous one who liked to get on with it. She was the one who made sure we were going the right way and doing the right things in the right places.

After a while, since Ruth was so busy and I was always the earlier riser in the house, I began to make breakfast for us. Eventually, it reached a point where I took over much of the cooking. Ruth worked in the office until I called her upstairs to eat. We had a very nice little arrangement, dividing the housework and the publishing work in a very happy fashion. Also, Ruth maintained a pretty heavy schedule as a docent at the National Gallery, so I actually had more free time than she did.[6]

But their pleasure in working together at home lasted for only three years. Early in 1987 Ruth began to exhibit symptoms of Alzheimer's disease. Bill recalls that she made a serious clerical error in the family checking account; this was so unlike her that he was at a loss to understand it. Then one day Ruth admitted having what she described to her husband as "blackouts" at the National Gallery.

Bill Stokoe was devastated. He channeled all his intellectual and emotional energy into learning as much as he could about Alzheimer's disease. "There were very bad times," he recalls. "When the disease was first coming on and we didn't know what was the matter, Ruth would fly off the handle and get angry. I'd get angry back. Even after Ruth was diagnosed, she would have violent episodes and the doctor finally prescribed Haldol. Ruth knew what she was losing; she was aware that her world was coming apart."[7]

Stokoe began to look at nursing homes for his wife but decided to care for her himself as long as he could. "After forty-five years," he says, "it was better for both of us to stay together for as long as possible."[8] With the same dedication he had applied to his work at Gallaudet, he made life for the two of them as satisfying and comfortable as he could. The onset of the disease

was particularly difficult, but within a year Ruth's violent episodes ceased and she no longer needed medication to sleep. She
became "the gentlest, sweetest, most tranquil person to look
after you could imagine," Stokoe says.[9]

In fact, Stokoe was able to find amusement in his wife's behavior:

> Half the time, when she gets out of bed at night, she
> doesn't let go of the cover and the down comforter but takes
> them with her. This morning I found one draped over the
> railing at the top of the stairs. Sometimes she takes it into the
> bathroom with her. So far I've been able to save it from
> getting dunked in the toilet bowl. Somewhere along the
> way — thank the Lord, to whom I've prayed about this — I
> learned to avoid losing my temper and blowing up and curs-
> ing or banging things around. I just see the humor in it and let
> it go.[10]

Stokoe sold his motorcycle soon after the illness was diagnosed, saying, "It wouldn't do either of us any good if I were
stuck in the hospital after a spill." He spent almost all of his time
with his wife.[11]

Ruth Stokoe's illness devastated the entire family. The terrible loss is apparent in a letter to Bill from his granddaughter,
Jennifer.

> Oh, I had the most vivid dream about Grandma a couple of
> nights ago. In my dream it was my wedding day . . . and I was
> getting ready to go down the aisle. Mom and my friends . . .
> were all helping me with the last-minute things. Then, I
> asked everyone to leave the room so I could be alone for a
> couple of minutes. Once they left, Grandma came bursting
> through the door asking, "Where's my granddaughter the
> bride?" Then she came over and hugged me, looked at my
> dress and said, "Oh, this will never do; take that dress off. I
> always told you you'd wear mine. There, now you're ready to
> go down that aisle. Take a look in the mirror." Then I turned
> to look at myself in the mirror and turned back to give
> Grandma a hug and she was gone. It startled me so much I
> woke up. I even walked around the apartment looking for

her. . . . That dream was so real it made me miss her even more.[12]

Nowhere is the suffering that Ruth Stokoe's illness caused her husband more apparent than in his account of finding two small slips of paper with her writing on them: "They are two of a great many little scribblings Ruth did in the fall and winter of 1987, when reason was snapping off and on like a light bulb almost at the point of finally burning out. The smaller slip was done, no doubt, when Ruth was looking at a catalog of paintings of the Niagara region. . . . The larger slip is even more heartbreaking. I can't tell if her word "angryness" is about her own occasional behavior or about my reactions to it. Lord, have mercy."[13]

Bill Stokoe's many friends began to worry about him. They insisted that he was working too hard, that at his age he should not have such enormous responsibilities, that he had no time for himself, that he had lost too much weight after having a pacemaker implanted in August of 1990. But Stokoe, in his quiet, stubborn way, continued to do exactly what he wanted to do. "There is no danger whatsoever that I will lose myself in serving Ruth," he said. "It's not so much serving her as continuing our life together and doing the things for her that she did for me and would do for me if I needed them."[14]

Early in 1992, after caring for his wife for five years, Stokoe found a nursing home nearby where he was sure she would be comfortable. The home was close enough that he could spend several hours with her every day. In November of that year, he had two dozen red roses delivered to Ruth in celebration of their fiftieth wedding anniversary. When he paid his daily visit that afternoon, he recalls, "Ruth was dozing in her chair right in front of the mantlepiece where the roses with my card were displayed. As I walked over to greet her by name, she opened those lovely blue eyes, focused a moment, and her whole face shaped into a smile."[15]

Just as Stokoe accepted the circumstances imposed by his wife's illness, he also came to terms with Gallaudet. Initially, he could barely talk about the closing of the lab, "it sickened me so."[16] He was angry enough to refuse the title of Professor

Emeritus when the school offered it to him in 1984. I. King Jordan recalls that "Bill . . . didn't leave feeling good about Gallaudet, and he didn't feel good about the way he perceived Gallaudet to feel about him."[17]

But several events softened Stokoe's attitude. The Deaf President Now Revolution in March of 1988 brought dramatic changes in the administration. In May of 1988, Jordan presented Stokoe with an honorary degree. Stokoe was also invited to speak at the Deaf Way Conference held at Gallaudet in the summer of 1989. All of this served to offset the treatment he had received earlier. Stokoe jokes about this, saying he's been "rehabilitated, like they used to do in Russia when old guys like Khrushchev reemerged."[18]

Jordan had consulted with Stokoe in 1988 about whether to apply for the presidency of Gallaudet. Stokoe had known Jordan for more than twenty years. When Jordan arrived at Gallaudet as an undergraduate (he majored in psychology), Stokoe was chairman of the English Department. Once Jordan overcame the "awe of being with such a distinguished scholarly gentleman who obviously knew everything there was to know," their friendship flourished. Jordan remembers asking for Stokoe's recommendation:

> The decision to apply for the presidency was one that I made after very, very serious soul-searching and careful study and review by me and my whole family. When I decided to go ahead and apply, I decided to get three people to write letters of recommendation. I wanted someone from my field . . . somebody who could write about what kind of research I had done and my work as a psychologist. I wanted a deaf person who was from the Deaf community and had the respect of other deaf people and could talk about my contributions to deaf society and deaf education. Finally, I wanted somebody who did scholarly work in the area of sign language. There was only one choice there.
>
> The decision to ask Bill to support my application for the presidency and write a letter of reference was easy. What really surprised and encouraged me was the response: he was delighted to do it. The letter that he wrote for me, wow!

What a wonderful letter. If I can measure up to what he said I have the potential to do, Gallaudet is really going to be a better place.[19]

Jordan applied for the presidency soon after Dr. Lee announced his decision to retire in 1987. However, in March of 1988, the Board of Trustees nominated Elisabeth Zinser as the next president. Jordan initially supported her appointment, but the students of Gallaudet refused to accept the board's choice. Not only was Zinser hearing, she knew no sign language. Within hours, the Deaf President Now Revolution began: a week-long event that captured the country's — and the world's — attention and admiration.

Stokoe remained at home with Ruth but kept his television on and watched anxiously as events unfolded. He describes how he felt that week:

When the revolution got to the point of demanding the resignation of the board chairman and the replacement of the current board with a majority of deaf members, I thought to myself, "Good Lord, I can't believe it's finally happening." It was something that I wanted so much to see that I was afraid to turn the television on in the morning for fear of discovering that the police or the national guard had been sent in to disperse the strikers. I wanted to know how it was going, yet I always feared that it would go badly for the good side. . . .

I was so heartened when I heard the student leaders being interviewed on television, with an interpreter voicing for them. I was reading their signs and knew what they were saying: "We want a president who knows and understands and appreciates our culture and language." Just that coupling of culture and language in there. You can't separate them. It wasn't just "sign language" that the students wanted, they wanted someone who understood the deaf experience, who participated in their likes and dislikes, their values, their customs, their beliefs. I felt very good at the end of that revolution.[20]

Even before Jordan became Gallaudet's first deaf president, Harry Markowicz (currently an English professor at Gallaudet) and David Armstrong (an anthropologist who also works at Gallaudet) had written to the Board of Trustees nominating Stokoe for an honorary degree. Markowicz had known Bill Stokoe for years, since being invited to the lab as a young scholar. Bill had been impressed with Markowicz's work and had published one of his papers in *Sign Language Studies*, a surprise to Markowicz because at the time he didn't have a master's degree. "I was so used to that academic mode that I was startled that Bill even took the time to read my work."[21]

Armstrong's work has also been published in *Sign Language Studies*, and he and Stokoe are close friends. They lunch together so often, Armstrong says, that "Bill and I are due permanent seats at Colonel Brook's Tavern."[22] Armstrong describes the circumstances that led to the nomination.

> Harry and I decided to nominate Bill for the degree [because] we were both distressed at the way he had been allowed to retire unrecognized, and we wanted to do something to repair the hurt that had been caused by the dissolution of the Linguistics Research Lab. At that time, we thought we would be proposing the degree to a board chaired by Jane Spilman and a university led by Jerry Lee. We were not at all certain of success, nor were we certain Bill would accept the degree if it were offered. We submitted our letter in December of 1987, along with supporting documentation.
>
> Bill's nomination was to be one of the items of business following the election of a new president at the board's March meeting the following year.[23]

Three months after the Deaf President Now Revolution in May of 1988, the day came for Stokoe to be awarded the honorary degree. He decided to bring Ruth with him. "Even if she couldn't know what was happening," he explained, "she belonged there with me."[24]

I. King Jordan remembers the occasion well; it was a fitting tribute for a lifetime of extraordinary dedication and accomplishment:

> I wanted Bill to know how Gallaudet felt about him. The response has been nothing but positive. Everywhere I go

people talk about the honorary degree and are delighted. People recognize the appropriateness of it.

Bill was, I believe, honored and pleased when he accepted the degree. I was emotional when I gave it to him. Ruth sat right in the front row right next to my wife. Ruth was becoming ill at that time with Alzheimer's disease. It was a very difficult time for Bill, and it was at the same time a wonderful time for him to receive the degree. I could see the struggle going on inside him. He received the degree, sat on the stage, but his heart and his mind in large part were down in that front row with Ruth.

It was a long ceremony. He actually had to leave before the ceremony was completely over. I thought it was a lovely thing to do. It was clear that Ruth needed him and it was clear that he belonged with her. He got up very quietly and very graciously walked off the stage, walked down and took his wife out of the audience to a place where she would be more comfortable. It was a very emotional time in my tenure as president.[25]

Armstrong recalls that Bill received a long standing ovation and that he "was genuinely pleased and gratified. I think the wound was at least partially healed."[26]

That same month, the Department of Linguistics and Interpreting at Gallaudet sponsored the second in a series of international conferences entitled "Theoretical Issues in Sign Language Research." Stokoe was asked to present a "historical perspective" on sign language research. He accepted the invitation, although he was still angry about the department's neglect of Baker-Shenk and Cokely. (Neither had been hired by Gallaudet after the closing of the lab. The department had, however, found a prominent place in its library for Stokoe's extensive collection of articles and books on sign language, rescuing it from the boxes in the corner.)

Stokoe's acceptance of the invitation reflected a softening attitude toward Gallaudet, but it also reflected his wish to maintain contact with others in his field. The opportunity to meet with and address a new generation of sign language researchers was irresistible. Calling his presentation "a personal view," he gave an account of his first exposure to sign language, his work with Trager and Smith, the creation of *Sign Language Structure*, and the compilation of the dictionary. He talked about *Sign Language Studies* and the people whose work he had published there. And he warned against the tendency among current researchers to ignore "the give-and-take of human interaction" in favor of "the fascinating and remote nooks and crannies of linguistic structure."[27] (It was this statement, among others, that led Carol Padden to wonder whether Stokoe was still "a part of the very modern discipline of sign language linguistics."[28]) Stokoe defended his position in the conclusion of his address:

> This view, that equal attention must be given to language, to the people who use it, and to what they use it for and about, has not impressed those who want to find in language a perfect, abstract system. It is a view that recent events have vindicated, however. Consider this: if sign language research in America had been directed solely at the internal structure of ASL, and if [only] a "standard model" grammar of all that linguists know [about it] were now in print, very few persons other than linguists would even know [ASL] existed. What has happened, however, as everyone . . . knows, is that in passionate defense of their own language and culture, deaf people have turned Gallaudet University around. What people fight for is their right to have their culture and their language respected, not the details of that language in the abstract.[29]

Despite Stokoe's enthusiasm, all is not well at Gallaudet. Lou Fant describes current conditions as follows:

> I don't think Gallaudet has ever appreciated what Bill did. They shoved him around, cut off funds for his research, and breathed a sigh of relief when he retired. Oh, they pay him lip service, but look at it. The university has yet to declare officially that ASL is the language of deaf people. . . . Gallaudet still does not require ASL fluency from its faculty. Look what happened to Carl Dupree. That could have been avoided had the security guards been fluent in ASL. [Dupree, a deaf Gallaudet student, was strangled to death in 1990 in a struggle

with Gallaudet security officers, who had handcuffed him — making it impossible for him to sign — and held him in a neck lock.]

Why should the college demand that students be fluent in English, yet not hold the faculty to the same standard with regard to fluency in ASL? It's disrespectful to deaf culture. Whatever prestige resulted from Bill's work must go to him, not to the university. Only George Detmold can officially represent the university when it comes to deserving praise. He supported and stood by Bill when no one else did.

People do not look to Gallaudet anymore for new information or research on ASL. There is no marker or monument on campus extolling Bill and his work. Gallaudet is out of the mainstream as far as ASL and deaf culture go. It didn't and still doesn't deserve Bill. He's too good for Gallaudet.[30]

Attitudes have begun to change at Gallaudet. In 1989 three Gallaudet researchers, Robert E. Johnson, Scott K. Liddell, and Carol J. Erting, published a 27-page document entitled "Unlocking the Curriculum." In it they make a strong argument for many of the same teaching practices that Stokoe had pleaded for in his 1975 memo to President Merrill about the education of deaf children.

While it may seem to be too obvious to say, it remains true that, in order to understand signed utterances built on English syntactic and morphological principles, a child must first be competent in English. It also remains true that most deaf children arrive at school with little or no competence in English. These observations combine to suggest that English is not the most appropriate language to use for instruction in important and valued parts of the curriculum. This conclusion seems to have escaped the reasoning of those who have designed our current approaches to instruction for deaf children.[31]

In the final paragraph of the document, the authors state their observations and predictions relative to the implementation of their recommendations. These comments are strikingly similar to those Stokoe made in 1975 when he asked President

Merrill to present his ideas to the Seventh Congress of the World Federation of the Deaf.

> The implementation of the proposals we are making will not be easy. It will require a long-term commitment of the educational resources of a large public school district or deaf school. In addition it will require, among other things: the recruitment of deaf teachers at the lower grades and preschool levels; retraining hearing teachers who do not sign well; community development work to establish various aspects of the parent-family program and the Child Development Center; a great deal of curriculum development; a great deal of materials development; and a program that teaches all participants in the program that the education of deaf children can be successful.[32]

In the summer of 1989, more than five thousand deaf people from all over the world attended The Deaf Way Conference, a combined festival and symposium, at Gallaudet. Bill Stokoe was asked to introduce anthropologist Edward Hall, the author of *The Silent Language* and *The Hidden Dimension*, and to give an address entitled "A Serious Sign Language Dictionary." Oliver Sacks, author of *Seeing Voices*, interviewed Stokoe at the conference (often referred to simply as "The Deaf Way"). "He is such an exceptional and warm human being," Sacks says, "one whose impact on linguistics, and the deaf, has been immeasurable. It was wonderful seeing him at The Deaf Way in 1989 — the Father of it all, enjoying the depth and rightness of appreciation which were denied him for so long."[33]

Sacks agrees with the critics of Gallaudet and other educational institutions that have chosen to ignore Stokoe's work and the growing field of research it engendered: "There are regressive or bigoted or plain inert traits in the education of the deaf which have completely ignored everything — the huge advances — of the last thirty years. So, paradoxically, Bill's work has — and has not — had an impact in some areas. No one who *knows* his work though, can be immune to it."[34]

It is no longer easy to ignore Bill Stokoe. In an essay entitled "The History of Language Use in the Education of the Deaf in the United States," Mimi WheiPing Lou creates a time line of "the major events [in the United States] pertaining to language use in the education of the deaf." Bill Stokoe's name appears at the point of acceleration in the shift from oral to manual communication, one hundred years after Bell's first advocacy of oralism and fifteen years before the Congressional passage of the Education for All Handicapped Children Act of 1975. (The act guarantees all children equal access to an education in the least restrictive environment appropriate to their particular needs.[35])

Bill Stokoe is flattered and amused by the attention he now receives. In May of 1990 the BBC aired a three-part series on language entitled "Born Talking," in which Stokoe, along with Carol Padden and Ted Supalla — two of the foremost deaf linguists in the United States today — was interviewed by Jonathan Miller. In July of 1991 Stokoe attended a convention of sign language interpreters, many of whom purchased the 1976 revised edition of his dictionary and asked him to autograph their copies. Stokoe notes, "We've come a long way from the time the original dictionaries were left in their shipping boxes in the basement of Gallaudet, being ruined by water dripping from the swimming pool above."[36]

Sue Livingston, an educator whose dissertation, "Levels of Development in the Language of Deaf Children," appeared in the Fall 1983 issue of *Sign Language Studies*, describes Stokoe as "our Trager and Smith." In this she represents the views of many educators, interpreters, and researchers in the field. Stokoe, she says, "articulated for us the observations we were making in our classrooms about language and learning as we taught deaf children in the early 1970s — observations the 'experts' kept telling us were wrong. He published articles in *Sign Language Studies* that were considered heretical by those in control of deaf education, but which gave us the confidence to realize that they were the ones who were wrong."[37]

Given Stokoe's current stature, readers of *Sign Language Studies* and other publications of Linstok Press often assume the press is a major operation complete with modern office facilities and a full support staff. Until recently, however, when the press moved to Sign Media, Inc., in Burtonsville, Maryland, Stokoe continued to work alone in the basement of his house.

"A nice thing happened to me this afternoon," Stokoe recalled a few months before the move.

> I was down in the basement packing copies of *Sign Language Studies* to send to subscribers when the phone rang. I just said as usual, "William Stokoe speaking." The caller was quite taken aback and said, "Oh my goodness, it's like finding Moses on the line." His name was Mike Cargo, an interpreter who wanted to get a subscription to *Sign Language Studies. . . .* We chatted for a few minutes. When I thanked him for his order, he thanked me for all the good things I had done for the profession. It was a very touching tribute.
>
> I'm always surprised by this kind of thing because for very long there didn't seem to be much of any indication that anyone was listening. I realize now a lot of the people teaching and interpreting weren't even born when I published *Sign Language Structure*. It's kind of hard to realize time passes like that.[38]

Knowing that Ruth Stokoe was well cared for, Bill was able to resume traveling. In September of 1992 he and David Armstrong flew to England to present a paper entitled "Gesture and the Origin of Syntax" at a meeting of the Language Origins Society in Cambridge. In October of 1992 Stokoe joined his best friend, George Detmold, at a testimonial dinner in honor of Gil Eastman, who was retiring after thirty years at Gallaudet. At the same time, Stokoe was completing two book manuscripts for publication early in 1993 and was well into the winter issue of *Sign Language Studies*. In November of 1992 he traveled to Copenhagen to deliver a lecture and to receive an honorary doctorate from Copenhagen University on its 455th anniversary — along with "a handshake and congratulations from Queen Margarethe, both regal and cordial in lovely purple, with a splendid plumed black hat."[39]

In 1993 Stokoe consented to serve on a task force on ASL and deaf studies at Gallaudet. But the task he found "most enjoyable" that year was typesetting the travel journals that Ruth Stokoe had kept for more than thirty years on all their trips together. In 1993 he had one hundred copies of the journal published privately and distributed them to family and friends.

Stokoe believed the book, entitled *Realms of Gold*, would be, "in my own biased opinion, a wonderful souvenir of the Ruth they know and love."[40] Family, friends, and colleagues agreed, purchasing every copy available.

In 1993 Stokoe was featured in a number of magazine and newspaper articles, among them *Smithsonian* magazine, the *New York Times* (a prominent mention), the *Chronicle of Higher Education*, and *Deaf Life* (a three-part article).

In February of 1994 Stokoe had lunch with Dorothy Casterline and her husband, Jim, and Carl Croneberg and his wife, Eleanor. "We all had a most wonderful time," he says. "It was as if the thirty years since we were working on the dictionary hadn't happened. It still astonishes me that I have so many friends in the Deaf world despite my lack of fluency in signing and worse skill at conversational ASL."[41]

Stokoe, David Armstrong, and Sherman Wilcox, a linguist, had been collaborating since 1992 on a book to be published by Cambridge University Press. Entitled *Gesture and the Nature of Language*, the book came out in 1994 and was widely acclaimed in the linguistic community. It is vintage Stokoe, combining the authors' research in their own fields with studies in biology, communication, and culture to prove that language cannot be understood apart from everything that makes us human. Stokoe feels that this book will be another step in the progress toward full recognition of American Sign Language.

> The real revolution has only begun. The revolution of 1988 put King Jordan in the university president's chair and made Phil Bravin chairman of its board; some state schools for the deaf now have Deaf superintendents; the public is intrigued instead of offended by the sight of someone signing. But all of this is only a slight change in direction. A complete revolution traverses 360 degrees. Ever since Samuel Heinicke argued that there is no real language without speech, experts and the public have trusted their own (limited) experience, ignored the testimony and examples of deaf people, and taken speech to be language, language to be speech.
>
> But Armstrong, Wilcox, and I read the evidence still coming in — from fossils to brain scans — as turning the revolu-

tion to full circle. Once (and perhaps still in some minds) it was believed that speech and language combining made hominids human. Consequently, sign languages were treated as irrelevant: teachers like E. M. Gallaudet found them helpful; speech specialists like Alexander Graham Bell called them pernicious. But when all the evidence is in, realization will dawn that language and humanity began with potent visible symbols. Gestures not only do the work of words; they express sentences with visibly connected parts. Thus they show, as spoken words never can, how complete thoughts were first formed. Instead of pitying, tolerating, or trying to change people who sign because they are deaf, science and the public will look more carefully at what signers do in order to *see* how their communication may give us clues to the way we became human.

I suppose this sounds radical, but so did what I said about sign language almost forty years ago. I really believe that modern science will change the neglect and mistreatment once the lot of deaf people not just to tolerance but to real respect, when it becomes better known how important vision and the neuromotor mechanisms are in the evolution of the human brain and its language and consciousness.[42]

Early in 1994, Stokoe sold the house that he and Ruth had lived in for almost fifty years and moved into an apartment built especially for him by his son and daughter-in-law in Chevy Chase, Maryland. In the midst of writing, reading, and editing he now can "travel just a few feet" to play with his grandchildren, Nathaniel and Madeline.[43] Each day, he visits his wife. "Ruth is holding her own," he says, "and I think she must enjoy the chair rides in the warmer weather, though it was sprinkling this morning so I read to her from her travel book — and, as always, came on a passage so poignant that I finished with wet eyes. 'Get a life,' they say nowadays. Well, I've had two or three: growing up in a loving family, a life of intellectual curiosity, and my life with Ruth — all three so satisfying that I can only marvel and give thanks."[44]

Stokoe confesses, however, to thinking occasionally about the things he hasn't accomplished.

Now that I'm going back over all this I realize that I would have liked more time to do the things I got started on but never became good at: gunsmithing, ham radio constructing and operating, boatbuilding (mostly repairing), engraving, sailing, cabinetmaking, flying (had my license renewed only once), gardening, tennis, racquetball, versifying. If the young deaf people carrying the ball now had only shown up twenty years ago, I could have left a lot of things to them and done more of my own.

Don't misunderstand — I'm not complaining. It's been a wonderful life and I have surely had much more than a normal share of satisfaction, joy, and delight. But there are still all those things I'd like to have done well.

Maybe there's still time. For what it's worth, my new accounting software, *Managing Your Money*, has a planning module based on life expectancy, and it tells me I should see ninety-three.[45]

Bill Stokoe celebrated his seventy-fifth birthday on July 21, 1994. That day, he addressed the Stanford Archimedes Project in Rochester, New York, visited friends, and then returned home to complete work on the fall 1994 issue of *Sign Language Studies*.

At this rate, Bill Stokoe may never get to concentrate on his many hobbies. But he probably won't mind that very much because, one suspects, in continuing his work with American Sign Language and the deaf community — an endeavor he began more than forty years ago — he is doing exactly what he wants to do.

NOTES

INTRODUCTION

1. Harlan Lane, ed., *The Deaf Experience: Classics in Language and Education* (Cambridge: Harvard University Press, 1984), 2.

2. Lou Fant, letter to the author, 1 May 1991.

3. Charlotte Baker and Robbin Battison, eds., *Sign Language and the Deaf Community* (Silver Spring, Md.: National Association of the Deaf, 1980), 32.

4. Fant, letter to the author, 1 May 1991.

5. William C. Stokoe, letter to the author, 6 June 1991.

6. Harlan Lane, letter to the author, 13 March 1991.

7. Stokoe, letter to the author, 20 November 1990.

8. Stokoe, letter to the author, 5 December 1990.

9. "Citation of William C. Stokoe, Jr., on Being Presented the Degree of Doctor of Letters, *Honoris Causa*, by Gallaudet University," 14 May 1988.

10. I. King Jordan, letter to the author, 28 May 1991.

CHAPTER ONE

1. Harlan Lane, *When the Mind Hears: A History of the Deaf* (New York: Vintage Books, 1984), 197.

2. Donald Moores, *Educating the Deaf: Psychology, Principles, and Practices* (Boston: Houghton Mifflin, 1978), 55.

3. Edward Miner Gallaudet, *History of the College for the Deaf, 1857–1907* (Washington, D.C.: Gallaudet College Press, reprinted 1983), 3.

4. Richard Winefield, *Never the Twain Shall Meet: Bell, Gallaudet, and the Communications Debate* (Washington, D.C.: Gallaudet University Press, 1987), 75.

5. Winefield, 109.

6. Gallaudet, 29.

7. Ibid., 21.

8. Ibid., 77.

9. *Thirteenth Annual Report of the Columbia Institution for the Deaf and Dumb (1870)* (Washington, D.C., Columbia Institution), 15.

10. Gallaudet, 243.

11. Ibid., 72.

12. Winefield, 94.

13. Ibid.

14. Edgar S. Weiner, *Official Report of The Convention of Articulation Teachers of the Deaf* (Albany, N.Y.: Voice Press, 1884), 4.

15. Ibid., 62.

16. Lane, *When the Mind Hears*, 393.

17. Winefield, 35.

18. Jerome Schein, *At Home Among Strangers* (Washington, D.C.: Gallaudet University Press, 1990), 26.

19. Alexander Graham Bell, *Memoir Upon the Formation of a Deaf Variety of the Human Race* (Washington, D.C.: Government Printing Office, 1884), 48.

20. Carol Padden and Tom Humphries, *Deaf in America: Voices from a Culture* (Cambridge: Harvard University Press, 1988), 57.

21. Schein, 148.

22. L. S. Vygotsky, *Mind in Society: The Development of Higher Psychological Processes* (Cambridge: Harvard University Press, 1978), 89.

23. Schein, 146.

24. Hans G. Furth, *Thinking without Language: Psychological Implications of Deafness* (New York: Collier-Macmillan, 1966), 13.

25. James Woodward, *How You Gonna Get to Heaven if You Can't Talk with Jesus: On Depathologizing Deafness* (Silver Spring, Md.: T. J. Publishers, 1982), 77.

26. Padden and Humphries, 112.

27. Schein, 147.

28. Helmer R. Myklebust, *The Psychology of Deafness: Sensory Deprivation, Learning, and Adjustment*, 2nd. ed. (New York: Grune and Stratton, 1964), xi.

29. Myklebust, 60, 68, 80, 87, 89, 107, 119, 123, 144, 145, 148–49, 157, 211.

30. Myklebust, 157, 158.

31. Myklebust, 159, 164–70.

32. Myklebust, 235, 171.

33. Myklebust, 190, 201, 211.

34. Myklebust, 219–20.

35. Myklebust, 228, 233.

36. Myklebust, 236.

37. Myklebust, 242.

38. Myklebust, 395, 396, 397.

39. Frank R. Zieziula, ed., *Assessment of Hearing-Impaired People* (Washington, D.C.: Gallaudet College Press, 1982), ix.

40. Padden and Humphries, 59.

CHAPTER TWO

1. Myklebust, 2.

2. Schein, 146.

3. Albert W. Atwood, *Gallaudet College: Its First One Hundred Years* (Lancaster, Pa.: Intelligencer Printing Co., 1964), 70.

4. Ibid., 72.

5. Ibid., 46.

6. Ibid.

7. Atwood, 47.

8. Ibid., 93.

9. Edward T. Hall, letter to the author, 2 April 1991.

10. Arden Neisser, *The Other Side of Silence* (Washington, D.C.: Gallaudet University Press, 1990), 41.

11. *Report of the Evaluation of Gallaudet College by the Middle States Association of Colleges and Secondary Schools*, Commission on Institutions of Higher Education (March 13 and 14, 1952).

12. Irving S. Fusfeld, "A Study of the Report of the Evaluation Committee of the Middle States Association of Colleges and Secondary Schools" (undated).

13. George E. Detmold, letter to the author, 19 January 1991.

14. Ibid.

15. Ibid.

16. Detmold, letter to the author, 25 January 1991.

17. Stokoe, letter to the author, 5 December 1990.

18. Detmold, letter to the author, 12 January 1991.

19. Padden and Humphries, 92.

20. Stokoe, letter to the author, 6 December 1990.

21. Stokoe, letter to the author, 13 November 1991.

22. Detmold, letter to the author, 25 January 1991.

23. Stokoe, letter to the author, 17 November 1990.

24. Henry Myers, *Are Men Equal? An Inquiry into the Meaning of American Democracy* (New York: Cornell University Press, 1945), 59.

CHAPTER THREE

1. Baker and Battison, 105.

2. Stokoe, letter to the author, 20 January 1991.

3. Mimi WheiPing Lou, "The History of Language Use in Education of the Deaf," in *Language Learning and Deafness*, ed. Michael Strong (New York: Cambridge University Press, 1988), 89.

4. Baker and Battison, 193–94.

5. Stokoe, personal communication, 5 December 1990.

6. Stokoe, personal communication, 3 January 1991.

7. Stokoe, personal communication, 19 January 1991.

8. William C. Stokoe, Dorothy C. Casterline, and Carl G. Croneberg, *A Dictionary of American Sign Language on Linguistic Principles* (Washington, D.C.: Gallaudet College Press, 1965), 297.

9. Jordan, letter to the author, 28 May 1991.

10. William C. Stokoe, *The Study of Sign Language* (Washington, D.C.: Center for Applied Linguistics, 1970), ERIC Document Reproduction Service No. HV 2474-S-74.

11. Carol Padden, letter to the author, 18 June 1991.

12. Stokoe, personal communication, 12 April 1992.

13. Baker and Battison, 12.

14. Ibid.

15. Detmold, letter to the author, 25 January 1991.

16. Robert Panara, letter to the author, 24 July 1991.

17. Panara, letter to the author, 18 August 1991.

18. Panara, letter to the author, 24 July 1991.

19. Padden and Humphries, 112.

20. Jerome Schein, letter to the author, 3 April 1991.

21. Jordan, letter to the author, 28 May 1991.

22. Stokoe, personal communication, 5 December 1990.

23. Panara, letter to the author, 18 August 1991.

24. Robbin Battison, letter to the author, 12 May 1991.

25. Stokoe, personal communication, 3 January 1991.

26. Stokoe, letter to the author, 23 January 1991.

27. Furth, 212.

28. Baker and Battison, 141.

29. Stokoe, personal communication, 12 December 1991.

30. Baker and Battison, 265.

31. Charlotte Baker-Shenk, profile of William Stokoe (1983).

32. Detmold, letter to the author, 13 January 1991.

33. Detmold, letter to the author, 25 January 1991.

34. Baker and Battison, 226.

35. *Report of the Evaluation of Gallaudet College by the Middle States Association of Colleges and Secondary Schools*, Commission on Institutions of Higher Education (February 10–13, 1957), 8.

36. Ibid.

37. Stokoe, *Sign Language Structure: An Outline of the Visual Communication Systems of the American Deaf*, Studies in Linguistics, no. 8

(Buffalo: Department of Anthropology and Linguistics, University of Buffalo, 1960).

CHAPTER FOUR

1. Stokoe, letter to the author, 11 May 1991.
2. Stokoe, letter to the author, 27 July 1991.
3. Padden and Humphries, 61.
4. Baker and Battison, 25.
5. Stokoe, personal communication, 28 February 1991.
6. Stokoe, letter to the author, 11 January 1991.
7. Stokoe, letter to the author, 1 February 1992.
8. James R. Newman, ed., *The World of Mathematics: A Small Library of the Literature of Mathematics, from A'hmose the Scribe to Albert Einstein,* 4 vols. (New York: Simon & Schuster, 1956).
9. Stokoe, letter to the author, 11 January 1991.
10. Ibid.
11. Stokoe, personal communication, 3 January 1991.
12. Ibid.
13. Stokoe, *Sign Language Structure,* 8.
14. Ibid.
15. Fant, letter to the author, 1 May 1991.
16. Stokoe, *Sign Language Structure,* 21.
17. François Grosjean and Harlan Lane, eds., *Recent Perspectives on American Sign Language* (Hillsdale, N.J.: Lawrence Erlbaum Associates, 1980), 7.
18. Stokoe, *Sign Language Structure,* 40.
19. Baker and Battison, 38.
20. Stokoe, *Sign Language Structure,* 51.
21. Stokoe, *Study of Sign Language,* 6.
22. Stokoe, *Sign Language Structure,* 7.
23. Ibid., 30.
24. Ibid., 3.
25. Strong, 89.
26. Baker and Battison, 18.
27. Ibid., 42.
28. William C. Stokoe, *The Calculus of Structure: A Manual for College Students of English* (Washington, D.C.: Gallaudet College Press, 1960), 17.
29. Carl G. Croneberg, letter to the author, 31 July 1991.
30. Robbin Battison, letter to the author, 12 May 1991.
31. Schein, letter to the author, 3 April 1991.
32. Fant, letter to the author, 1 May 1991.

33. Panara, letter to the author, 18 August 1991.
34. Fant, letter to the author, 1 May 1991.
35. Detmold, letter to the author, 21 January 1991.
36. Ibid.
37. Fant, letter to the author, 31 January 1991.
38. Battison, letter to the author, 12 May 1991.

CHAPTER FIVE

1. William C. Stokoe, "Structural Linguistics and the Language of the Deaf" (a speech addressed to the Washington Linguistics Club, Washington, D.C., October 1960).
2. Gordon Hewes, letter to the author, 28 March 1991.
3. Thomas S. Kuhn, *The Structure of Scientific Revolutions* (Chicago: University of Chicago Press, 1962), 67.
4. Baker and Battison, 139.
5. Baker-Shenk, profile of William Stokoe, 4.
6. Baker and Battison, 267.
7. Ibid., v.
8. Tom Humphries, letter to the author, 20 May 1991.
9. Harlan Lane, letter to the author, 13 March 1991.
10. Humphries, letter to the author, 20 May 1991.
11. Stokoe, letter to the author, 28 February 1991.
12. Stokoe, personal communication, 8 April 1991.
13. Hall, letter to the author, 2 April 1991.
14. Jordan, letter to the author, 28 May 1991.
15. Stokoe, letter to the author, 3 January 1991.
16. Stokoe, personal communication, 27 January 1991.
17. Stokoe, letter to the author, 15 January 1991.
18. James Woodward, personal communication, 4 June 1991.
19. Battison, letter to the author, 12 May 1991.
20. Schein, letter to the author, 3 April 1991.
21. Padden, letter to the author, 18 June 1991.
22. Baker and Battison, 20.
23. Ibid., 19.
24. Croneberg, letter to the author, 20 May 1991.
25. Croneberg, letter to the author, 6 August 1991.
26. Croneberg, letter to the author, 20 May 1991.
27. Dorothy Casterline, letter to the author, 31 May 1991.
28. Stokoe, letter to the author, 7 August 1991.
29. Detmold, letter to the author, 14 August 1991.
30. Baker and Battison, 54.
31. Baker and Battison, 41.
32. Stokoe, letter to the author, 4 August 1995.

33. Battison, letter to the author, 12 May 1991.

34. Casterline, letter to the author, 31 May 1991.

35. Stokoe, Casterline, and Croneberg, *Dictionary of American Sign Language*, xii.

36. S. Stasheff, review of *A Dictionary of American Sign Language on Linguistic Principles*, by Stokoe, Casterline, and Croneberg, *Language Learning* 16, nos. 3–4 (1965).

37. Baker and Battison, 195.

38. Ibid., 32.

39. Ibid., 194.

40. Stokoe, Casterline, and Croneberg, *Dictionary of American Sign Language*, 301–6.

41. Croneberg, letter to the author, 14 August 1991.

42. Baker and Battison, 207.

43. Stokoe, letter to the author, 7 August 1991.

44. Stokoe, personal communication, 3 January 1991.

45. Ibid.

46. Virginia Covington, personal communication, 6 June 1991.

47. Stokoe, letter to the author, 8 January 1991.

48. Detmold, letter to the author, 12 August 1991.

CHAPTER SIX

1. Detmold, letter to the author, 8 May 1991.

2. Ibid.

3. Stokoe, letter to the author, 17 December 1990.

4. Panara, letter to the author, 18 August 1991.

5. Edward C. Merrill, Jr., letter to the author, 6 March 1991.

6. Detmold, letter to the author, 16 March 1991.

7. Stokoe, personal communication, 15 January 1991.

8. Stokoe, letter to the Honorable Albert H. Quie, 13 November 1970.

9. Michael Karchmer, personal communication, 8 August 1991.

10. Casterline, letter to the author, 14 April 1993.

11. Stokoe, letter to the author, 17 July 1991.

12. Neisser, 46.

13. Woodward, personal communication, 4 June 1991.

14. Covington, personal communication, 6 June 1991.

15. Stokoe, memorandum to members of the English Department, Gallaudet University, 23 March 1971.

16. Covington, personal communication, 6 June 1991.

17. Minutes, meeting of the English Department, Gallaudet University, 13 April 1971.

18. John Schuchman, personal communication, 11 June 1991.

19. Stokoe, personal communication, 15 January 1991.

20. Schuchman, personal communication, 11 June 1991.

21. Baker and Battison, 143.

22. Stokoe, personal communication, 15 January 1991.

23. Stokoe, undated memorandum to Gallaudet University Department of Safety and Security.

24. Stokoe, letter to the author, 22 June 1991.

25. Ibid.

26. Stokoe, letter to the author, 22 April 1991.

27. Merrill, letter to the author, 6 March 1991.

28. Woodward, personal communication, 4 June 1991.

29. Jordan, letter to the author, 28 May 1991.

30. Battison, letter to the author, 12 May 1991.

31. Padden, letter to the author, 18 June 1991.

32. Charlotte Baker-Shenk, personal communication, 22 June 1991.

33. Lane, letter to the author, 13 March 1991.

34. Edward Klima and Ursula Bellugi, *The Signs of Language* (Cambridge: Harvard University Press, 1979), vii.

35. Baker-Shenk, personal communication, 22 June 1991.

36. Stokoe, personal communication, 20 June 1991.

37. Battison, personal communication, 12 May 1991.

38. Woodward, personal communication, 4 June 1991.

39. Dennis Cokely, personal communication, 18 February 1991.

40. Covington, personal communication, 6 June 1991.

41. Stokoe, letter to the author, 12 December 1990.

42. Stokoe, letter to Dr. Laszlo Stein, 23 June 1975.

43. Lane, letter to the author, 13 March 1991.

44. Ibid.

45. Fant, letter to the author, 1 May 1991.

46. Stokoe, letter to the author, 27 January 1991.

47. I. M. Schlesinger and L. Namir, eds., *Sign Language of the Deaf* (New York: Academic Press, 1978), 367.

48. Stokoe, *Study of Sign Language*, 10.

49. William C. Stokoe, "An Untried Experiment: Bicultural and Bilingual Education of Deaf Children" (proposal submitted to Edward C. Merrill, Jr., national chairman of the Seventh Congress of the World Federation of the Deaf, March 1975).

CHAPTER SEVEN

1. Stokoe, letter to the author, 20 August 1991.

2. Ibid.

3. Ibid.

4. Ibid.

5. Ibid.

6. Baker-Shenk, personal communication, 20 August 1991.

7. Cokely, personal communication, 28 February 1991.

8. Harry Markowicz, personal communication, 5 June 1991.

9. Battison, letter to the author, 12 May 1991.

10. Stokoe, letter to the author, 4 June 1991.

11. Virginia Volterra, letter to the author, 13 May 1991.

12. Leon Auerbach, letter to the author, 2 February 1991.

13. Merrill, letter to the author, 6 March 1991.

14. Padden, letter to the author, 18 June 1991.

15. Battison, letter to the author, 12 May 1991.

16. Woodward, personal communication, 4 June 1991.

17. Stokoe, personal communication, 22 June 1991.

18. Woodward, personal communication, 4 June 1991.

19. Volterra, letter to the author, 13 May 1991.

20. William C. Stokoe, ed., *Sign and Culture: A Reader for Students of American Sign Language* (Silver Spring, Md.: Linstok Press, 1980), 290–91.

21. William C. Stokoe, "Where Is Language Evolution Getting Us?" (paper presented at the annual conference of the Niagara Linguistics Society, Sanborn, N.Y., March 1977).

22. William C. Stokoe, "Linguistics and Anthropology in Sign Language" (paper presented to the Cambridge University Linguistics Department, Cambridge, England, October 1977).

23. Stokoe, personal communication, 15 January 1991.

24. Baker and Battison, 140.

25. William C. Stokoe, "Sign Language Research: What It Knows and Whither It Goes" (paper presented at BDA/NCSD [British Deaf Association/Northern Counties' School for the Deaf] Workshop, Newcastle, England, October 1977).

26. Neisser, 54–55.

27. Lane, letter to the author, 13 March 1991.

28. Ibid.

29. Baker and Battison, vii.

30. Baker-Shenk, personal communication, 7 June 1991.

31. Gil Eastman, personal communication, 8 May 1991.

32. Sherman Wilcox, ed., *American Deaf Culture: An Anthology* (Silver Spring, Md.: Linstok Press, 1989), 24–25.

33. Stokoe, letter to the author, 5 December 1990.

34. Stokoe, *Sign and Culture*, 2.

35. Wilcox, 169.

36. Ibid., 168.

37. Stokoe, personal communication, 22 June 1991.

38. Ibid.

39. Detmold, letter to the author, 18 June 1991.

40. Volterra, letter to the author, 13 May 1991.

41. Stokoe, note to Virginia Volterra, 6 July 1982.

42. W. Lloyd Johns, letter to Gallaudet University community, 4 January 1984.

43. Stokoe, letter to the author, 28 February 1991.

44. Schein, letter to William Stokoe, 27 May 1983.

45. Ursula Bellugi, letter to W. Lloyd Johns, 15 July 1983.

46. François Grosjean, letter to W. Lloyd Johns, 7 June 1983.

47. Hewes, letter to W. Lloyd Johns, 4 June 1983.

48. Lane, letter to W. Lloyd Johns, 3 June 1983.

49. Johns, form letter to supporters of the Linguistics Research Laboratory, 31 August 1983.

50. *On The Green*, 26 November 1984, 1.

51. *Buff and Blue*, 7 December 1984, 1, 5.

52. Ibid., 5.

53. Baker-Shenk, personal communication, 7 June 1991.

54. Doin Hicks, memorandum to Raymond J. Trybus, 9 September 1983.

55. Ibid.

56. Dennis Berrigan, letter to W. Lloyd Johns, 21 June 1983.

57. Barbara Kannapell, letter to W. Lloyd Johns, 1 September 1983.

58. Anne Fadiman, letter to W. Lloyd Johns, 17 June 1983.

59. Padden, letter to the author, 18 June 1991.

60. Baker-Shenk, personal communication, 7 June 1991.

61. Ibid.

62. Covington, personal communication, 6 June 1991.

CHAPTER EIGHT

1. Jordan, letter to the author, 28 May 1991.

2. Stokoe, personal communication, 8 April 1991.

3. Humphries, letter to the author, 20 May 1991.

4. Jordan, letter to the author, 28 May 1991.

5. Lane, letter to the author, 13 March 1991.

6. Stokoe, personal communication, 5 December 1990.

7. Ibid.

8. Ibid.

9. Ibid.

10. Ibid.

11. Stokoe, personal communication, 3 January 1991.

12. Jennifer Phillips, letter to William Stokoe, 19 August 1991.

13. Stokoe, letter to the author, 16 February 1991.

14. Stokoe, letter to the author, 8 April 1991.

15. Stokoe, letter to the author, 27 November 1992.

16. Stokoe, letter to the author, 22 June 1991.

17. Jordan, letter to the author, 28 May 1991.

18. Stokoe, letter to the author, 5 June 1991.

19. Jordan, letter to the author, 28 May 1991.

20. Stokoe, personal communication, 4 December 1990.

21. Markowicz, personal communication, 15 April 1991.

22. David Armstrong, letter to the author, 15 April 1991.

23. Ibid.

24. Stokoe, personal communication, 8 April 1991.

25. Jordan, letter to the author, 28 May 1991.

26. Armstrong, letter to the author, 15 April 1991.

27. Ceil Lucas, ed., *Sign Language Research: Theoretical Issues* (Washington, D.C.: Gallaudet University Press, 1990), 6.

28. Padden, letter to the author, 18 June 1991.

29. Lucas, 7.

30. Fant, letter to the author, 1 May 1991.

31. Robert E. Johnson, Scott Liddell, and Carol Erting, *Unlocking the Curriculum: Principles for Achieving Success in Deaf Education*, Gallaudet Research Institute Working Paper 89–3 (Washington, D.C.: Gallaudet University, 1989), 7.

32. Johnson, Liddell, and Erting, 23.

33. Oliver Sacks, letter to the author, 19 March 1991.

34. Ibid.

35. Strong, 78.

36. Stokoe, letter to the author, 24 August 1991.

37. Sue Livingston, personal communication, 3 June 1991.

38. Stokoe, personal communication, 8 April 1991.

39. Stokoe, letter to the author, 27 November 1992.

40. Stokoe, personal communication, 1 April 1994.

41. Stokoe, personal communication, 2 February 1994.

42. Stokoe, letter to the author, 9 May 1995.

43. Stokoe, personal communication, 6 August 1994.

44. Stokoe, letter to the author, 21 April 1995.

45. Stokoe, letter to the author, 5 May 1992.

INDEX

CPSIA information can be obtained
at www.ICGtesting.com
Printed in the USA
FFOW02n1912130418
46229777-47577FF